How To Become
A Crime Scene
Investigator

www.How2Become.com

As part of this product you have also received FREE access to online tests that will help you to become a Crime Scene Investigator.

To gain access, simply go to:

www.MyPsychometricTests.com

Get more products for passing any test at:

www.How2Become.com

Orders: Please contact How2Become Ltd, Suite 14, 50 Churchill Square Business Centre, Kings Hill, Kent ME19 4YU.

You can order through Amazon.co.uk under ISBN 978-1911259329, via the website www.How2Become. com or through Gardners.com.

ISBN: 978-1911259329

First published in 2017 by How2Become Ltd.

Copyright © 2017 How2Become.

Typeset by How2Become Ltd.

Disclaimer

Every effort has been made to ensure that the information contained within this guide is accurate at the time of publication. How2Become Ltd is not responsible for anyone failing any part of any selection process as a result of the information contained within this guide. How2Become Ltd and their authors cannot accept any responsibility for any errors or omissions within this guide, however caused. No responsibility for loss or damage occasioned by any person acting, or refraining from action, as a result of the material in this publication can be accepted by How2Become Ltd.

The information within this guide does not represent the views of any third party service or organisation.

Contents

Chapter 1 *The Role*..3

Chapter 2 *Core Competencies*.........................17

Chapter 3 *The Application Form*......................31

Chapter 4 *The Telephone Interview*.................53

Chapter 5 *CSI Assessment Centre*..................67

Chapter 6 *Assessment Centre Interview*........147

Chapter 7 *Final Interview*...............................173

Chapter 8 *A Day in The Life of a CSI*..............205

Chapter 9 *Helpful Organisations*....................215

Hello, and welcome to *How To Become A Crime Scene Investigator.* In this book, we're going to teach you all about how to become – you guessed it – a crime scene investigator.

Now, if you've ever watched TV, you might be carrying some preconceived ideas on what a crime scene investigator actually is, and what they do on a daily basis. While the media representation of 'CSI' isn't always too far off, there is far more to the job of a crime scene investigator than you are probably aware of.

Let's start off with the basics. Here is a quick fact list of things you need to know about becoming a crime scene investigator:

- Crime scene investigators are also known as 'scenes of crime officers';

- Crime scene investigators attend all kinds of crime scenes, not just murder. This includes burglary, sexual assault and arson;

- Crime scene investigators are required to wear a uniform. The dark shades and suits that you see on TV are not accurate;

- Crime scene investigators are often required to attend horrific and devastating scenes. As a result, they need to be emotionally prepared for this;

- Crime scene investigators are required to have excellent photography skills.

Now that we've cleared up a few myths about the role,

here's an overview of how this book is structured.

In this guide, we'll give you a comprehensive overview of everything that you need in order to become a crime scene investigator. With the help of insider experts, we'll take you through the entire process: from application stage to assessment centre, interview to medical check-up. Along with this, we'll also provide you with numerous tips and tricks to help you master your investigatory technique and impress your future employer. By the end of this book, you will be perfectly placed to apply for a job as a crime scene investigator!

Let's start by looking at what the role entails.

Chapter 1
The Role

The role of a crime scene investigator is extremely varied. However, as the name suggests, the main body of your work will be spent directly investigating crime scenes. This means that you'll have to attend, in person, and perform tasks such as:

- **Ensuring that the crime scene is free from potential contamination.** It's particularly important to ensure that evidence doesn't get cross contaminated. Cross-contamination occurs when evidence is mixed up with other evidence, or gets moved by people visiting the scene. Investigators wear gloves to prevent contamination from happening, and crime scene tape is placed around the area in question.

- **Preserving and collecting key pieces of evidence.** It's extremely important to ensure that evidence is protected and maintained in exactly the same condition that it was found. For this reason, investigators use plastic containers/bags, in which they place each piece of evidence.

- **Taking photographs of the crime scene.** Crime scene photography is a really important part of the process. It documents the appearance of the crime scene, the victims, and the position of key pieces of evidence – such as footprints and blood patterns. It provides a permanent visual record of the scene, which can then be used in the investigation/as evidence.

Now, as we mentioned in the introduction, this is nowhere near as simple as it sounds. It's pretty tough to collect key pieces of evidence, especially when you are in the same room as a deceased victim. You've probably never tried taking a fingerprint sample from a man who has been bludgeoned to death with a hammer, but it takes nerves of steel. If you want to be a crime scene investigator, you need to be someone who is able to manage your emotions in situations such as this. At times the job will be extremely unpleasant, and you'll see things that you wish you hadn't, but you'll need to keep a cool head and carry on with your task. For this reason, it's fair to say that crime scene investigation isn't for everyone.

For a good example of how keeping your cool can impact on your ability to do the job, try the following:

Get hold of a friend, and ask them to look at a photograph containing 4 or 5 people. Let them look at the photograph for 1 minute, then take it away. Don't tell them why you are asking them to look, and don't even give them warning that you are going to ask them. Just put them on the spot. Then start asking them questions about the photo, such as:

• What colour hair did the boy on the right have?

• How many people were sitting down?

• What colour was the bus in the background?

You'll probably find that they are extremely shocked, and as result, miss out on loads of details. Their memory has been impacted by fear and surprise. This is a good example of why you need to learn to control your emotions. If you let them get the better of you, then this could prevent you from doing your job to the best of your ability.

Murder is just one of the crimes that investigators deal with on a regular basis. Crime scene investigators are not just limited to fatal incidents, but also attend many other criminal investigations. You will frequently need to attend scenes involving burglary, rape or arson. Just as before, you will need to cast a precise eye over every single detail at the scene, collecting and preserving evidence.

The normal working pattern of a CSI involves working approximately 40 hours per week, including weekends. You will generally work as part of a shift system, and can be called upon at any time of the day or night, meaning you have to be prepared to make social sacrifices. You'll start each day at the police station, and from there will travel to crime scenes. Crime scene investigators work in many different types of weather, so be prepared to get your hands dirty when required! Rain is no obstacle for a CSI.

Once CSIs have collected evidence, they are then responsible for evaluating the significance of this evidence, and sending off this evidence to the police lab. Anything from small fibres to tiny amounts of bodily fluid can be sent off for analysis, and then used to charge suspects.

When attending a crime scene, investigators will look for physical evidence, including:

• Fingerprints;

- Footprints;

- Glass;

- Hair;

- Blood;

- Liquid.

They'll then bag or preserve these pieces of evidence, before sending them back to the lab for testing and analysis.

DID YOU KNOW?

There are 43 home police forces in England and Wales, 8 in Scotland and one national Police Service in Northern Ireland.

Along with all this, crime scene investigators don't just attend crime scenes, but also spend periods of time working back at or outside of police HQ. Here, they are required to complete important tasks such as:

- Producing written reports;

- Assisting other members of the investigatory team;

- Attending courts and giving evidence;

- Participating in evidence based searches, such as zone searches and grid searches.

Now, let's look at certain things which could really help you to get the job.

What do I need to become a Crime Scene Investigator?

The requirements to become a CSI will vary from force to force. While some constabularies won't officially require you to have a degree in forensics, photography or criminology, this will almost certainly help your cause. CSI jobs are extremely popular, and you can expect that a large number of the candidates applying will be in possession of degrees. In fact, more and more constabularies are now asking their candidates to have some kind of forensic or photographical degree to their name, prior to application. The more qualified you are for the role, the better you will stand out during the application process, and the more likely you are to be successful.

The good news is, there are an enormous number of CSI jobs generally available. Although the competition is fierce, this means that there are a huge variety of places to which you can apply. With 43 police forces in the UK, you won't be short of options. The biggest employer, of course, is the Met Police in London. CSIs also work for smaller regional forces, and for the British Transport Police. Once employed as a CSI, you will be required to take part in National Police Improvement Agency (NPIA) training, and take a refresher course in CSI once every 5 years.

If the constabulary that you are applying for does require you to have a degree, then you will probably need:

- A degree in a science-related subject, such as biomedical or forensic science.

OR

- A Higher National Certificate/or Diploma in photographic studies.

Forensic science in particular is a very popular degree course. To get onto these courses, you will generally need to have a minimum of at least 2 A-Levels, with one being a science-based subject.

Along with this, you will also need:

- A full valid UK driving license;

- An excellent standard of eyesight.

Both of the above are fundamental requirements for any CSI. CSIs must be able to drive to and from crime scenes, often on very short notice. You may be asked to take a basic driving assessment prior to application, to prove your capability behind the wheel. Likewise, having good eyesight is essential, as you need to be able to spot small details at the scene.

Once you do obtain a job as a crime scene investigator, you'll generally start off as an assistant. You'll then be mentored/work alongside a more experienced colleague, who will help you get to grips with the role.

As a new CSI, you can expect to take enormous amounts of training. The NPIA runs established training courses for new CSIs, which teaches them the fundamentals of concepts such as digital photography, evidence collection, fingerprint analysis, crime scene reports and health and safety. The courses are run in conjunction with your on-the-job training, and will eventually lead to you receiving a foundation degree in crime scene investigation.

Now, before we move onto the core competencies for the job, let's take a brief look at the structure of the police. This will help with your wider knowledge, and could prove useful in the interview.

The Police Structure

The UK Police Service is made up of many different ranks. Starting from the bottom, everyone who joins the police as an officer, will undergo a probationary period which usually lasts for two years. During this time, you must pass continuous training assessments and demonstrate to your superior officers that you have what it takes to become a fully qualified police officer.

When you join your chosen constabulary, you will be immediately issued with a number. This number is more commonly known as your warrant number. The warrant number stays with police officers for the entirety of their service, and all the way up to the rank of Sergeant. You will wear this number on your uniform shoulders whilst on duty. If you get promoted past the rank of sergeant, then this number will no longer appear on your uniform.

Sergeant is the first promotion after the rank of police officer. In order to become a sergeant, you will need to pass a number of examinations. These exams are nationally run, and include assessments such as the OSPRE. In order to progress beyond the role of

Sergeant, you will need to seriously dedicate yourself to the force, as well as taking significant amounts of extra training.

Now, let's look at the Police Rank Structure in more detail.

Chief Constable – This person is responsible for the running of their Police Service, and reports directly to the elected members of the Police Authority.

Deputy Chief Constable – This person acts as the deputy to the Chief Constable, and will also run the force when he or she is on leave/or away on duties outside of the Police Force.

Assistant Chief Constable – This person is usually responsible for a specific section of the Police Force, such as Operations and Intelligence.

Chief Superintendent – This person is responsible for policy of a large area or Command of the Police Force in that area. These are usually geographical.

Superintendent – The Superintendent is usually responsible for a section of a Borough or Command, such as Operations, Crime or Partnerships.

Chief Inspector – These people usually oversee large teams; such as response teams, CID or investigations. They are responsible to the Chief Constable for their particular area.

Inspector – Oversees all officers who are on duty at any given time, 24/7. Inspectors are operational and will also attend and take charge of serious operational incidents.

Sergeant – These supervise a team of officers at a station or unit. You will also see 'Custody Sergeants' at police stations in this role.

Police Constable – Generally turn up and respond to 999 calls. They will also gather information at incidents in their log books and attend court to give evidence when required.

Along with this, here are some of the different Crime Scene Investigator ranks/specialities:

Senior Investigating Officer (SIO): The SIO is the person who is in charge of the overall management of a crime scene investigation. This person decides on what direction to take in regards to evidence collection, forensic strategy, etc. They will usually have a deputy, known as a **Deputy SIO.**

Major Crime Forensic Adviser (MCFA): This person is tasked with coordinating the forensic support for a crime scene investigation. They are responsible for managing the forensic strategy, liaising with the forensic department and representing the SIO in regards to forensic matters.

Crime Scene Manager (CSM): A Crime Scene Manager is an individual who is tasked with managing individual crime scenes. They will act under the instructions of the SIO and MCFA, to make certain that every forensic angle is covered, and that the scene is managed in an appropriate manner.

Crime Scene Investigator (CSI): As you've probably

gathered from our book, Crime Scene Investigators are responsible for examining crime scenes, recovering evidence and then sending it back to the lab for further analysis. CSIs can also branch out into other specialist CSI fields, such as photography.

Scene Log Officer (SLO): The Scene Log Officer is responsible for maintaining an accurate and in-depth crime scene log, and assisting with the control of the crime scene area.

Bloodspatter Analyst: Bloodspatter analysts examine blood that is left behind at crime scenes. They use different techniques to collect evidence from the scene, which will later be used in the investigation. These techniques include taking photographs and using ultraviolet light. The pattern and position of the blood at the crime scene can tell investigators an enormous amount about what has occurred, and can even be used to confirm or refute statements made by suspects/ witnesses.

Forensic Photographer: Forensic photographers are responsible for, you guessed it, taking photos of crime scenes. These photos can later be used in court, and are analysed during the investigation. Forensic photographers need to take photos of everything at the scene, including fingerprints, footprints, bullet holes and other important evidence. They are also required to take detailed photographs of injuries and victims, including dead bodies.

Ballistics Expert: Ballistics experts specialise in analysing anything to do with firearms. For example, they will analyse specific bullets or weapons, identifying the trajectory of bullets, the type of weapon used, etc. They do the bulk of their work in the lab, but may also attend crime scenes themselves.

Educational Routes

The level of education that you will need in order to enter the field, will generally depend on the career that you are thinking of specialising in. For example, if you are thinking of working directly in the lab, then you'll almost always be required to have at the very least a degree. As we have mentioned though, in order to become a CSI, there are no official educational requirements. That being said, more and more constabularies are asking for their crime scene investigators to have a degree or more before applying; and you can fully expect that a large number of the candidates who are applying will have these degrees. School or university qualifications in subjects such as chemistry will give you a big edge. Likewise, maths and computer science will also be extremely useful.

Work Experience

Work experience is always a useful thing to have on your application. Many constabularies will require their candidate to have some experience in forensics or of working in a laboratory based environment. Obviously, it's not always easy to gain work experience in these environments, given the specialist demands involved. However, any form of forensic or laboratory-based experience – whether voluntary or paid, including working at university or even volunteering at school, will be helpful. Previous work experience in the police force will also be extremely useful, and some police forces have schemes which allow candidates to volunteer.

Likewise, some degree programmes offer their students a year working within the industry. These programmes are linked with agencies or forensic providers, allowing students to gain exposure to the industry prior to applying for jobs. This will provide you with great experience to use on your application form, and could even get you a job working with the company if you impress them.

As we have mentioned, the competition for these jobs is fierce, so it's important that you are able to distinguish yourself from the other candidates. Work experience will help you to do that.

Chapter 2
Core
Competencies

Just as with any job, in order to become a crime scene investigator, you will need to adhere to a strict set of behavioural guidelines. These are known as core competencies, and learning them is one of the most important things you can do in order to gain a job. Whether you are applying to the role, or working as a crime scene investigator, you will need to demonstrate these competencies over and over again in order to be a success. The competencies aren't just a guideline for you to follow, they are a huge part of why the police are respected by the public.

There are two sets of competencies to pay attention to here. The first, is the national police competencies. Even though you are working as a crime scene investigator, you are still employed by the police, and therefore it's fundamental that you have a good understanding and knowledge of these competencies. You will need to learn them off by heart, in order to pass the application process. Throughout the application process, you will need to use these competencies on a constant basis. Below we've run through the national police core competencies, and given you a brief overview of what qualities they encompass.

National Police Core Competencies

Public Service

Demonstrates a real belief in public service, focusing on what matters to the public and will best serve their interests. Understands the expectations, changing needs and concerns of different communities, and strives to address them. Builds public confidence by talking with people in local communities to explore their viewpoints and break down barriers between them and the police. Understands the impact and benefits of policing for different communities, and identifies the best way to deliver services to them. Works in partnership with other agencies to deliver the best possible overall service to the public.

Openness To Change

Positive about change, adapting rapidly to different ways of working and putting effort into making them work. Flexible and open to alternative approaches to solving problems. Finds better, more cost-effective ways to do things, making suggestions for change. Takes an innovative and creative approach to solving problems.

Service Delivery

Understands the organisation's objectives and priorities, and how own work fits into these. Plans and organises tasks effectively, taking a structured and methodical approach to achieving outcomes. Manages multiple tasks effectively by thinking things through in advance, prioritising and managing time well. Focuses on the outcomes to be achieved, working quickly and accurately and seeking guidance when appropriate.

Professionalism

Acts with integrity, in line with the values and ethical standards of the Police Service. Takes ownership for resolving problems, demonstrating courage and resilience in dealing with difficult and potentially volatile situations. Acts on own initiative to address issues, showing a strong work ethic and demonstrating extra effort when required. Upholds professional standards, acting honestly and ethically, and challenges unprofessional conduct or discriminatory behaviour. Asks for and acts on feedback, learning from experience and developing own professional skills and knowledge. Remains calm and professional under pressure, defusing conflict and being prepared to step forward and take control when required.

Decision Making

Gathers, verifies and assesses all appropriate and available information to gain an accurate understanding of situations. Considers a range of possible options before making clear, timely, justifiable decisions. Reviews decisions in the light of new information and changing circumstances. Balances risks, costs and benefits, thinking about the wider impact of decisions. Exercises discretion and applies professional judgement, ensuring actions and decisions are proportionate and in the public interest.

Working With Others

Works co-operatively with others to get things done, willingly giving help and support to colleagues. Is approachable, developing positive working relationships. Explains things well, focusing on the key points and talking to people using language they understand. Listens carefully and asks questions to clarify understanding, expressing own views positively and constructively.

Persuades people by stressing the benefits of a particular approach, keeps them informed of progress and manages their expectations. Is courteous, polite and considerate, showing empathy and compassion. Deals with people as individuals and addresses their specific needs and concerns. Treats people with respect and dignity, dealing with them fairly and without prejudice regardless of their background or circumstances.

Along with the above competencies, there are also crime scene investigator specific competencies. While these aren't as important during the initial application process, you will still be expected to use and demonstrate your knowledge of them, and they will be extremely important when it comes to the final interview.

DID YOU KNOW?

The first recorded use of fingerprint evidence, in an English court, was in 1902.

Crime Scene Investigator Core Competencies

Attention To Detail

Attention to detail is one of the most fundamental skills that a crime scene investigator must have. When attending a crime scene, it is your job to spot and identify often tiny pieces of evidence, which untrained eyes might not have noticed. Very often, the key to solving a crime is in the tiny details; a stray hair, a misplaced fingerprint, a loose fibre. The better you can spot these details, the better you will be at your job. Along with this, you'll need to be taking detailed notes on everything that you spot. You'll need to take notes on elements such as:

• The presence of blood at the scene, and the areas in which it was and wasn't present.

• The position of bodies.

• The initial impression of the crime scene, before any markers or investigatory tools have been placed.

If the crime scene is outside, then you will need to take immediate steps to establish which pieces of evidence could be compromised by the elements, such as hairs or clothing fibres, and then collect this evidence as a matter of priority.

Along with this, it's also important that crime scene investigators are astute and accurate in measurements. When taking notes, you'll need to ensure that distances and measurements are written down, for example, noting how far blood was found from the victim. This ensures that the locations of important evidence can be used later in the investigation.

Communication and Teamwork

On the face of it, it might seem as if communication wouldn't play a big part in the role of a crime scene investigator. However, it's actually really important for a crime scene investigator to have fantastic communication skills. When investigating, you will be part of a team, along with other investigators, lab technicians and police officers. You will all need to work together to solve the case, and discuss evidence together. It's also imperative that you can communicate with people whom you haven't met before, as you will often find yourself visiting crime scenes alone, without a colleague. On top of this, you may also need to communicate with people who have been the victim of a crime, so it's important that you can deal with these people in a sensitive and diplomatic manner.

As a crime scene investigator, one of your primary tasks upon arriving at the scene is to get it cordoned off, to ensure that evidence is free from disruption. This means that you must clearly indicate your requirements to the other officers, as they will need to follow your investigatory protocol. Along with this, crime scene investigators are sometimes required to attend court, to act as witnesses; as they are fantastically placed to provide the jury with vital logistical information.

It's not just verbal communication that is important either. When working as a crime scene investigator, you will need to be able to call upon good written skills too. Investigators are constantly taking notes on the things that they see, and often will be required to produce case reports, which can later be used in court.

Organisation

When working as a crime scene investigator, your organisation skills will be fundamental. There are so many essential things that a crime scene investigator will need to take care of, that you absolutely must ensure that you are on top of things and have your work in order. Disorganisation in this job could be disastrous, and could leave evidence exposed to contamination or inaccuracy.

Along with all of this, you'll need to take an organised approach to every case that you have worked on, ensuring that you have a detailed record of every single investigation. Remember that your organisation skills aren't just for the benefit of you, but for the entire crime solving investigation.

Composure

Composure is a big part of this job. You need to be someone who can remain calm under pressure, and you must be able to handle distressing and difficult situations. This is really hard, especially when you are required to deal with a deceased victim, or a particularly gruesome crime scene. This is something that you will be taught how to deal with during your training for the role, but you still need to be able to demonstrate this quality during the application process. It's imperative for the police that you are someone who can handle this, because they don't want to employ someone who will get as far as their first crime scene and then realise that it's too much to deal with. It's important to note: crime scene investigation is not for everyone. You have to be particularly strong to handle many elements of this job. The calmer you can remain, the better you will be able to do the job, and the sharper your investigatory skills will be.

Analytical Skills

In order to be a crime scene investigator, you must have strong analytical skills. Crime scene investigation isn't just about routinely inspecting and detailing the scene of a crime, it's about analysing what you have found, to help the police come to conclusions about the crime. This skill will be evident in your case reports, and your work back at the station. As a crime scene investigator, nobody is expecting you to solve crimes all by yourself, but your input to the case goes far beyond simple note taking. Crime scene investigators are an integral part of the team. Throughout the application process, you can expect to make full use of your analytical abilities, which will be tested to the limit – especially at the assessment centre.

Accuracy

Accuracy is incredibly important for crime scene investigators. Inaccuracies can derail an entire investigation, so it's vital that you are razor sharp when taking notes and photographs. This ties in with almost all of the other competencies, since you need to be accurate in absolutely everything that you do. The small details that you can spot, will form the platform on which the police build the whole investigation, so it's essential that you get the details right. Anything from the position of a body to the location of a blood spot on the wall can make the difference – the small details really count, and it's your job to ensure that these details are accurate.

As you might have guessed, these competencies will be essential when working in the role. For this reason, they will also be really important during the application process. At every single stage of the application process, you will need to demonstrate these competencies as much as you possibly can. The assessors will score you based on how much you meet and have demonstrated the core requirements of the role, in your verbal answers and written answers.

Applying For The Role

In this book, we'll give you an extremely detailed overview of the application process for becoming a crime scene investigator. Now, however, let's take a brief overview of what the process actually involves.

To apply for a job as a crime scene investigator, you will need to apply directly through the constabulary that you are looking to work for. So, if you want to become a crime scene investigator for the Kent Police, you'll need to apply through the Kent Police website. Remember though that there may not be a vacancy in your constabulary, so keep a close eye out for similar positions which open up in nearby areas.

The number of stages that you'll have to take when applying to become a crime scene investigator will depend upon the constabulary to which you are applying. Each constabulary will have a different way of doing things, and could require you to attend extra stages than another might ask you to. In this book, we'll take you through every single stage that you may be asked to take as part of your application process. Before applying, you should check with your constabulary as to what the recruitment process is.

The stages that you will likely have to take are:

- **Application Form.** This is something that every constabulary will require you to take. On this form, you will need to provide the force with details such as your personal information, your criminal record and your work/education history. Finally, you may be required to answer a series of competency-based questions. In the next chapter, we'll cover this in great detail.

- **Further Application Form.** For some constabularies, you will be required to fill in a further application form. If you do have to fill in this form, then you will almost certainly have to answer competency-based questions. Some constabularies will use the initial application form as a personal/vetting check, before asking candidates who pass this stage to answer a competency-based form.

- **Telephone Interview.** Some constabularies might ask you to pass a telephone interview. This will take place after the application form stage, and will require you to speak with someone from the constabulary on the phone, for around half an hour. Later in this guide, we'll give you some top tips on how to ace this.

- **Assessment Centre.** Next, you'll have to attend an assessment centre. Some constabularies will ask you to do this, while others won't. You'll attend the assessment centre with many other candidates, and will complete a series of tests, based around the requirements of a crime scene investigator. Finally, you'll finish off the day with an interview. The interview at the assessment centre will be a controlled interview. This means that you'll have

4 questions, with 5 minutes exactly to answer each question. The questions will be centred on the national police core competencies.

- Final Interview. The next (and final) stage that you have to attend, is a final interview. The final interview will be much longer than your previous interview, and will be slightly less informal. You'll be given a wide range of questions, not just competency questions. If you reach this stage, then you can be assured that the constabulary are extremely interested in hiring you.

- Medical/Physical Checks. Finally, once you've passed all of this, you'll need to attend a medical and physical check up with the constabulary. In particular, they will pay close attention to the quality of your eyesight. Good eyesight is a fundamental requirement for a crime scene investigator to have.

- Further training. Finally, once you have been accepted into the force, you will need to go through a period of extensive training. This will be mixed with on-the-job experience, and will aim to sharpen vital investigatory skills, such as photography and preventing evidence contamination.

In order to pass all of these stages, you will need to conduct extremely thorough preparation. It's really hard to become a crime scene investigator, and for good reason. Crime scene investigators play an incredibly important role in police operations, and therefore the police need to make sure that they have the right person for the job.

In the next chapter, we'll start looking at the application process. We'll begin with the application form.

Chapter 3
The Application
Form

In order to apply to become a crime scene investigator, you will need to apply directly through the constabulary to which you would like to work. You can either look for vacancies on your local police website, or – if there aren't any CSI vacancies at your local constabulary – a quick internet search should bring up any vacancies available around the country. Let's look at a typical job advertisement for a crime scene investigator:

Job Title: Crime Scene Investigator – Level 1/2

Location: Ficshire Police Headquarters, Crime Response Unit

Salary: £21,500 per annum

Job Type: Permanent

We are looking for a crime scene investigator, to work within our crime response unit. For this position, we are happy to consider both experienced and inexperienced crime scene investigators. The individual in question will be required to complete tasks such as undertaking forensic examination of evidence-based objects – such as vehicles, burglary scenes and stolen property. After a year's experience, you will progress to acting as a photographer at forensic post-mortems. Candidates will start at Level 1, and after completing 18 months of relevant experience, will progress to Level 2. During your first year, you will be required to complete a competency-based portfolio, as well as completing examinations from the college of policing. After a 6 month period in which it is agreed that you have performed satisfactorily, you will be required to attend a College of Policing course, which will help you on the way to achieving Level 2. During your first year, your working hours will usually consist of shift patterns, between 8am to 6pm.

Applicants for the position must possess at least 4 GCSEs, including English Language or Literature and Maths; or an equivalent. You must be in possession of a full current driving license, and will need to pass a basic driving assessment with the constabulary prior to being offered the position. You should refer to the Ficshire Police website for our policy regarding tattoos, piercings and criminal record. In addition to this, applicants to this job must have been a resident of the UK for at least 3 years prior to application.

Please note: Ficshire Constabulary has a strict vetting process. Any offer of employment will be subject to our standard vetting levels, which will be upheld/maintained throughout your employment.

The successful candidate will be expected to:

- Conduct investigation and examination of vehicles, burglary scenes and evidence related property.

- Take photographs at crime scenes, including post mortem and injury related photographs.

- Liaise with the police forensics department on a regular basis, helping with investigations.

- Assist in preparing exhibitions for court presentation.

- Attend court and give evidence when required.

- Work a dedicated shift rota, covering 7 days a week.

- Produce grammatically correct and accurate written crime scene reports, which can be used throughout investigations.

So, now that you've looked at a sample job description, let's study how to break this down into smaller pieces.

DID YOU KNOW?

The majority of police forces use a system called 'Livescan', to electronically scan fingerprints of people who are arrested.

As we have mentioned, the core competencies are essential when applying to become a crime scene investigator. At every single stage of the process, you will need to demonstrate and use these core competencies in your responses. If you break down the above job description, you should be able to see how the core competencies are relevant to every aspect. For example:

'To conduct investigation and examination of vehicles, burglary scenes and evidence related property'

In order to do this, you will need to utilise your **decision making**. You will also need to have fantastic **accuracy** and **attention to detail.**

'To take photographs at crime scenes, including post mortem and injury related photographs'

In order to do this, you will need to utilise your **composure,** your **attention to detail**, and your **accuracy.**

The same applies for all of the other core expectations

that we have listed above. So you see, even if the application form is not directly asking you for these competencies, you will be expected to read between the lines and form your answers accordingly. Now, let's look at a sample application form, to give you some idea of what to expect.

The Crime Scene Investigator Application Form

As we mentioned earlier, this form will differ depending on the constabulary that you are applying to. Every single form will ask similar vetting questions, such as your name, age etc. However, where constabularies may differ, is in the competency-based questions. Some constabularies may ask you to complete a series of competency based questions on the initial application form, but other constabularies may leave this out of the initial form, before sending you another form to complete later, once they have established that you meet their entry/eligibility requirements. Either way, at some point over the 1 or 2 forms, you will need to complete a series of competency-based questions. For the purposes of this book, we have broken our own section down into two parts. First, we'll focus on the vetting questions, and then we'll look at the competency questions.

The typical crime scene investigator application form will look very similar to the following:

Part 1: Personal Information

Please fill out the following personal details as accurately as you can. Please note, all of these details will be checked and confirmed during our vetting process. If you are successful in being appointed, any incorrect information could lead to termination of the employment process.

Title:

Forename:

Middle Name:

Surname:

Country of Birth:

Date of Birth:

Are you over the age of 18?:

Address details:

Town/City:

Country:

County:

Postcode:

Date of occupancy:

Mobile telephone number:

Home telephone number:

Email address:

National Insurance number:

Current salary:

Please state your nationality:

Please confirm that you are a British citizen or an EU member passport holder:

Additional Information

Please provide any dates in the next few months upon which you are categorically unavailable to interview. If this doesn't apply, state N/A:

Upon appointment to this role, I understand and agree to have my fingerprints and DNA taken, and held on record, for the purposes of elimination:

Are you currently employed, in any capacity, by Ficshire Police?

Do you have any family or close relationships with any person currently working within Ficshire Police?

Have you ever served or are you currently serving within another constabulary?

Are you a member of the BNP or any similar organisation, whose objectives might be construed to contradict the police values of racial equality?

Criminal History

In this section, you must declare if you have ever been the subject of a police investigation, or if you have been arrested, detained, charged, cautioned or convinced of any offence, by any UK or non-UK law enforcement. Please note, past or current convictions could have a significant impact on your chances of success: This includes:

- Any traffic offences, excluding parking penalties.

- Any receipt of an absolute/conditional discharge or bind over.

- Any receipt of a reprimand, warning or caution, obtained as an adult or as a juvenile.

- Any Anti-Social Behaviour Order, Football Spectator Banning order, Sexual Harassment charges or general harassment orders.

Please state whether you have any of the following:

- Are you currently the subject of an impending prosecutions?

- Are now currently involved in, or have you ever been involved in, any criminal investigation?

- Have you ever been the subject of disciplinary military action?

- Have you ever been involved in any action which could be deemed as politically/religiously/racially or environmentally damaging?

Financial Position

In order to work within the police, you will need to have a clean financial record. With this in mind, please answer the following questions:

*   I understand and consent that financial checks will be undertaken to verify my financial records, during the vetting process.

*   Have you ever had a loan agreement terminated, by the lender?

*   Have ever been the subject of an adverse court judgement, related to financial matters?

*   Have you ever been registered as bankrupt?

*   Have you ever been the subject of a repossession proceeding?

Tattoos

Ficshire Police have a very strict policy on tattoos. Please answer the following questions:

*   Do you have any tattoos on your hands, neck or face? If yes, please describe their nature, and upload a photo of the tattoo below.

*   Do you have any tattoos on your forearms? If yes, please describe their nature, and upload a photo of the tattoo below.

Language Skills

- Is English your first language? If not, please specify your first language.

- Please list any other languages in which you are proficient, and your level of fluency.

- Are you fluent in British sign language?

Previous Residence

If you have lived in more than one residence over the last five years, please list all of these addresses, starting with the most recent. You do not need to include your current address.

Employment

In this section, you will need to fill out all of your current and past employment details, including the reasons for why you left that position.

Education and Qualifications

In this section, you will need to fill out information on all of the schools/colleges/universities that you have attended since the age of 14. This will include providing your grades and qualifications that you have attained, as well as any extra training that you have undertaken.

Competency Questions/Essential Criteria

Now, we come to the most important part of the application

form. As mentioned, some constabularies will require you to fill this in as part of the main form, while others will ask you to submit your first form, and then send you a competency-based questionnaire. Either way, the questions that you encounter will be highly similar.

So, what are competency-based questions? Let's take a look at a typical question.

> *'In 200 words or less, please explain to us how organised you are, and why this would make you a good candidate for the role.'*

As you know from the opening chapters of this book, organisation is one of the core competencies of a crime scene investigator. A competency based question is a question which requires the candidate to not only demonstrate that they have this competency, but also to show that they understand why it's important for the role. Be careful, because some questions might not be as black and white as the above. For example, you might just be asked, 'Please explain to us how organised you are'. When answering this, you will still need to show that you understand why it's essential for the role, even if the question doesn't directly ask you to. Where possible, you will also need to give brief examples, which back up your point. This is great practice for later in the process. Once you reach the interview stage, you will need to give in-depth and detailed examples of when you have demonstrated each core competency, so this brief exercise should get you prepared for that.

When answering a competency-based question, make

sure you stay on topic. This is especially important when you are given a word limit, as you need to make every single word count. Structure your response so that it is easy to read, and easy for the assessor to establish that you meet their criteria. Below we've constructed a sample response to this question. Take a look at this, and then have a go at the other sample competency-based questions that we have listed. Don't forget to go back to the competencies listed at the start of the book, if you get stuck.

Q. 'In 200 words or less, please explain to us how organised you are, and why this would make you a good candidate for the role.'

A. I am an extremely organised and efficient person, and I believe that this quality (amongst others) makes me ideal for the role. Throughout my career, and my education, I have worked in positions which required both organisation and attention to detail. As the shift leader at my local fast food restaurant, I was required to keep a close eye on all of my staff members, and manage both their time and my own, effectively. By using my organisation skills, I ensured that the restaurant ran smoothly, and customers were always satisfied. I know that organisation is key for this role. Crime scene investigators deal with enormous amounts of critical information, and therefore it's essential that they have their work in order, and can take an organised approach to investigation. The more organised a CSI is, the better they can support the rest of the law enforcement team with solving crime. I also understand that crime scene investigators will sometimes need to present evidence in court. This alone makes organisation fundamental, and to this end, I am someone who would really suit this position.

There is also a good chance that you will be given a question that asks something similar to, 'Tell us what qualifications you have that make you ideal for this role' or 'tell us what has motivated you to apply for this position'. In these questions, you will need to combine your knowledge of the core competencies with your research of the role.

Further Sample Competency Questions

Q. In 200 words or less, describe your team working abilities, and why they are important for this role.

Sample Response

I am a really teamwork-orientated person, with a big focus on achieving team goals. Throughout my career, I have worked in professional teams, on many occasions as a leader, and therefore I am highly experienced in this area. This was most evident in my previous job at a financial advice company, where I led a team of 7 people to extremely impressive results. Working together, under my leadership, we managed to break several company monthly records. This was down to the unity and quality of communication between all of the members of our team. I understand that teamwork is extremely important for a crime scene investigator, as CSIs will need to work with many other law enforcement professionals to help solve crimes. Of course, I am completely happy and capable to work alone and without assistance, but I firmly believe that the power of the collective is far greater than that of just one individual. For this reason, teamwork is essential when working as a crime scene investigator, and therefore I am perfect for the role.

Q. In 200 words or less, tell us about what qualifications and experience you have, that makes you an ideal candidate for this role.

Sample Response

I believe that I have a great number of qualifications, which make me suitable for this role. First of all, I have extremely high grades in both Maths and English. I know that CSIs must be able to produce high quality written reports, which can be used in further investigation, and in court. Likewise, CSIs must be mathematically astute, able to calculate distances and the positions of objects at a crime scene.

Secondly, at university I achieved a degree in forensic science. This is something that has prepared me greatly for being a crime scene investigator. It taught me an appreciation for the importance of the smaller details, and the significance of things that other people might not spot at a crime scene. I also have a keen interest in photography, which I know links closely with CSI work.

Finally, I have undertaken two periods of work experience, assisting fully qualified crime scene investigators in their day-to-day professional lives. This gave me a fantastic insight into the type of organisational and methodical approach that CSIs need to take; and as a result, I believe that I am fully prepared for this role.

Q. In 200 words or less, tell us about your attention to detail.

Sample Response

I am someone with fantastic attention to detail, and I have demonstrated this throughout my career. This was particularly the case when I was studying for my forensic science degree. Naturally, this course required students to be as vigilant and attentive as possible. I excelled in this course, achieving top marks and a first degree. I then used this attention to detail in my career up until this date, utilising my accuracy whilst working for a financial support company. I know that the skills I have picked up here, will be absolutely fundamental when working as a crime scene investigator. It is imperative that CSIs have the ability to notice the smaller details of a case.

Q. In 200 words or less, explain what has motivated you to apply to become a crime scene investigator with this force?

Sample Response

There are many things which have motivated me to become a crime scene investigator.

Firstly, I want to be able to make a difference in the criminal justice field. I know that crime scene investigators can make a huge difference to the outcome of criminal investigations, and I would welcome the chance to be so influential in this field. I'm a very analytical person, with a keen interest in crime and puzzles, so I think that this job would suit me perfectly.

Secondly, I am really inspired by the work done by your constabulary. Having lived in this area for a long time now, I have benefitted from the protection and security that Ficshire Police provide to residents, and can say that I really admire and respect your officers. For this reason, I would absolutely love the opportunity to work as a part of your force.

Finally, I feel that I would be the perfect fit for the role. Having taken a forensic science degree, I am well equipped to deal with intricacies and requirements of this job, and believe that I would make an outstanding addition to your law enforcement team.

Chapter 4
The Telephone
Interview

Once you've submitted your application form, you will face a short waiting period to find out if you have been successful. Then, you'll be contacted by someone from your local constabulary, asking you to take part in a telephone interview. It should be noted that not all constabularies will use this system, and some might send you straight to the assessment centre after evaluating your application form. Regardless, you should be prepared to take a telephone interview, as this is great practice for the final interview later in the process. In this chapter, we'll explain what the telephone interview involves, and the best way to answer the questions.

What is a telephone interview?

As you can imagine, police jobs are extremely popular. Even if the constabulary that you are applying to is small and local, you can almost guarantee that they will have hundreds upon hundreds of applicants for the role. This means an awful lot of applications to sift through. Naturally, the police can't send every single person who applies to the assessment centre – as there simply wouldn't be room. With this in mind, it's important that they can sift out candidates who might not be right for the role. A telephone interview can last between 5 and 20 minutes, but is far more cost effective and efficient than screening hundreds of applicants at an assessment day. In essence, a telephone interview is a sifting process.

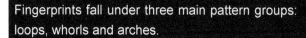

DID YOU KNOW?

Fingerprints fall under three main pattern groups: loops, whorls and arches.

Unfortunately, due to this, many candidates don't really take telephone interviews particularly seriously. They want to get to the next stage as quickly as possible, and start readying themselves for the all-important face to face interview. This is a huge mistake. If you want to reach the next stage, you need to fully prepare for the telephone interview.

What does the Crime Scene Investigator telephone interview focus on?

The CSI telephone interview is focused around competency-based questions, and gauging your motivation for working with the police. This means that your interview will actually be fairly similar to what you will experience in the actual physical interview stage, or indeed any interview for that matter. While you will be expected to have a good knowledge of the role, and the core competencies, there won't be any questions particular to 'phone interviews' that you have to watch out for.

That being said, be careful. Due to the fact that they aren't physically face to face with the interviewers, many people relax too much. They answer the phone while lying in bed, or watching TV. This is a HUGE mistake. In order to do your best at a phone interview, you need to find a quiet place where you can sit, listen and respond calmly to the questions being asked. Numerous studies have shown that your body language can dramatically affect your phone persona. In order to ensure you give the best impression to the interviewer, you need to be in the right place to do it.

During a telephone interview, the employer will not really be able to assess your 'likeability' factor, or whether or not you will fit into their team and organisation. However, a telephone interview is perfect for assessing whether or not you have the right skills, qualities and experiences for the job. I've personally interviewed hundreds of people for different jobs in the past, and sometimes I have thought to myself – "What the heck are you doing here?" It would have been far better for that person to have a telephone interview, because they clearly don't have the skills, attributes or qualifications to carry out the role. Furthermore, while an application form is a great way of assessing people, it doesn't involve any physical interaction with the person writing it. This can make it very difficult for assessors to ascertain whether that person is suitable.

How do you know whether or not you have the skills and experience they are looking for?

Earlier in this book, we provided you with a sample job description, and way to break the job description down into competencies. As a refresh, here are the crime scene investigator competencies again:

- Attention to detail;

- Communication and Teamwork;

- Organisation;

- Composure;

- Analytical Skills;

- Accuracy.

In order to be successful in your phone interview, or indeed any interview, you need to be able to demonstrate the core competencies through clear and relevant examples. Below, we have listed a number of sample questions that you could expect from the CSI phone interview, along with descriptions on how to answer these. This should help you to understand how you can use the competencies in your own responses to the questions.

To further aid you, make sure you use the **STAR method**:

The **STAR** method works most effectively when preparing responses to situational type interview questions. It ensures that your responses to the interview questions follow a concise and logical sequence and also makes sure that you cover every possible area.

Situation – At the commencement of my response, I will explain what the situation was and who else was involved. This will be a relatively comprehensive explanation so that the interviewer fully understands what it is I am trying to explain.

Task – I will explain what the task was. This will basically be an explanation of what had to be done and by whom.

Action – I will then move on and explain what action I specifically took, and also what action other people took.

Result – I will finally explain what the result was following my actions. It is important to make sure that the result was positive as a direct result of your actions.

Using this method not only shows your thought process for each response, but it allows you to take the time and think carefully about each step in the process of your response.

The competency-based questions from the application form are a great starting point to help you prepare for the telephone interview questions. Remember that since this interview effectively takes the form of a conversation, you will likely be asked to expand on specific points.

Example Questions

Below, we have laid out a typical series of CSI telephone interview questions, along with some tips on how to answer them. Later in this guide, we'll provide you with a dedicated interview chapter, where we provide you with full sample responses to all of the below questions, and many more.

> *Could you tell me about why you have applied for the role of a Crime Scene Investigator?*

One of the aims of the telephone interview is for the police to gauge your interest in the role. This doesn't have to be a lengthy response, just make sure that a) you convey a genuine interest and give good, logical reasons for wanting to work there, and b) match your response with what was put on the application form. In order to ensure you do this, print off your application form prior to sending it off, and then have a copy next to you when you are speaking to the interviewer. Remember to keep your answer sensible. For example, an answer that lists 'I want to see dead bodies' or 'I like the uniform' as reasons for wanting to work as a crime scene investigator is unlikely to impress the interviewer. Keep your answer short, concise and realistic. Try to show the interviewer an awareness of current events that the police are dealing with.

> *What do you know about the role, and what is it about this role specifically that attracts you?*

In this question, the interviewer is looking for confirmation that you understand the requirements of the role, and some indication that you have performed research into exactly what the role involves. Working as a crime scene investigator is often difficult and stressful, and you will be under large amounts of pressure, as well as being exposed to horrific scenes. Therefore it's really important that you know exactly what you are applying for. Remember that one of the core competencies is organisation. If you have not bothered to research the position by this point, then it is likely that you are not the type of person that the police want working for them. You can also impress the interviewer by showing knowledge of other roles within the organisation, and highlighting why the role you have chosen is the best fit for you.

Can you elaborate more on why you think this role would suit you?

This is a great question, as it allows you to elaborate upon and go into detail about the skills you have introduced in your previous answers. Later in the interview, you can give specific detailed examples of how you match the competencies. Here, you should give a brief outline of examples of when you have used your skillset to your advantage, and how you believe it could be used when working for the police.

What is your biggest weakness?

When answering this question, be careful. The worst answer that you can give here is, 'I don't have any weaknesses'. This will show a lack of self-awareness to the interviewer. They need to see that you are someone who recognises that there are always improvements to be made, and that you believe the police are the best organisation to help you do that. Obviously, don't reel off a big list of weaknesses here. The key is to pick 1 weakness, and try to put a positive spin on it. For example, you could tell the interviewer that you sometimes struggle to delegate work, because you are a perfectionist. As long as you make sure to tell the interviewer that you are working on solving this issue, this will show them that you are someone who prioritises attention to detail and good work, over rushed and sloppy assignments.

> *Give me an example of a time when you have had to prioritise assignments? How did you go about doing this.*

This is a good example of a competency-based question. Here, you are expected to demonstrate the core competency of organisation. Using the STAR approach, as outlined in chapter 3, give a problem-solution-resolution answer to this question. Make sure you tell the interviewer in clear detail about how the problem was fixed as a result of your actions, and you could even incorporate what you learned from the experience.

> *Give me an example of a time when you have faced criticism? How did you deal with this.*

When working as a crime scene investigator, you will be operating under highly pressurised conditions. Therefore, it's vital that you are someone who is able to use criticism constructively, in order to improve yourself. Everyone makes mistakes, the key is to learn from your mistakes and produce better results next time. If you can show the interviewer that you recognise this, you will stand a greater chance of passing the interview. Finish your example by showing the interviewer how your actions as a result of the criticism that you faced are now much better, and that you have improved yourself. Not only does this show an ability to learn and better yourself, but it also displays the core competency of working with others.

Give me an example of a time when you have had to work as part of a team to solve a problem.

In this question, you are being asked to demonstrate the core competency of teamwork. Part of working as a member of a team also involves using some of the other core competencies that the police are looking for, such as: good communication and organisation. Finally, this question is indirectly questioning your own composure and analytical abilities, as the question is specifically referring to the way in which **your** actions benefitted the team. Once again, make sure you use the STAR method to show how you went about solving the issue.

Give me an example of a time when you have had to use your analytical skills to solve a problem.

This question focuses specifically around the core competency of analysis, but could also involve attention to detail and accuracy. Along with this, in order to solve difficult problems, you will have to take an organised and efficient approach. Analytical thinking is absolutely key to working as a crime scene investigator, and will be a frequent part of your daily professional life. In your answer, you should show a willingness to take initiative, and emphasise your attention to detail.

Give me an example of a time when you have taken a flexible approach to solving problems.

This question is essentially asking you to demonstrate that you are someone who is able to adapt their priorities according to the seriousness of the problem that they are dealing with. When you are working as a crime scene investigator, you might be juggling a range of different projects at once. Thus, you need to have a flexible and adaptable approach. You must be able to prioritise issues according to their current status, rather than just the order in which you started working on them.

In chapter 7 of this guide, you will find sample responses to the above and many more interview questions. Below, we've included a list of top general tips for passing a phone interview.

10 important tips for passing any telephone interview:

TIP NUMBER 1

When you have a date for your telephone interview, immediately place it in your diary. You should then start preparing immediately for it. Most people prepare the night before the telephone interview, which is not particularly good practice! You have a lot of work to do, so the sooner you start the better. The areas that you need to work on are:

• How you communicate on the telephone;

• Researching the role you are applying for (you can do this by getting a copy of the job description or person specification).

TIP NUMBER 2

Before the telephone interview commences, make sure that:

- Your telephone is fully charged (if using a mobile phone);

- You are in an area that has a good reception (if using a mobile telephone);

- You will not be disturbed by anyone or anything.

TIP NUMBER 3

When the police calls you to undertake the telephone interview, make sure you speak clearly and concisely. Although the interviewer cannot see you, they will form an opinion of how you communicate. Communicating effectively includes:

- Speaking clearly and concisely;

- Being professional at all times;

- Avoiding the use of abbreviations or slang;

- Listening to what the interviewer has to say and answering the questions appropriately.

TIP NUMBER 4

It is far better to be seated comfortably in a quiet room away from any distractions during the telephone interview. Some people prefer to stand up and walk around; however, if you do this you are likely to breathe heavily during the interview, which may be distracting to the interviewer.

TIP NUMBER 5

If you have previously submitted an application form

prior to the telephone interview, make sure you have a copy of it in front of you. It is also advisable that you have a copy of your CV. This way, if the interviewer asks you questions about your previous employment or qualification dates, then you will have the information to hand.

TIP NUMBER 6

Have a pen and piece of paper in front of you so that you can write down notes and even briefly write down any questions they put to you, so that you can refer back to them during questioning.

TIP NUMBER 7

It's useful to have a glass of water to hand during a phone interview (but move the phone away from your mouth when you swallow). You will be doing a lot of talking and you don't want your mouth to dry up at a crucial moment during the telephone interview.

TIP NUMBER 8

Be sure to smile when speaking during the telephone interview. You would be amazed at the difference it makes to your tone of voice. Even though they cannot see you, they will hear a positive vibe in your voice if you smile whilst you speak!

TIP NUMBER 9

During a face-to-face interview, you interact with the interviewer by nodding your head and showing facial expressions. Obviously you cannot do this during a telephone interview. Therefore, you have to show that you are paying attention by using small phrases and communicational confirmations such as "OK", "uh-huh", "I see", "I understand", "yes" or similar quotes/phrases.

TIP NUMBER 10

A large part of the telephone interview assessment will be how you communicate. Communicating effectively is not just about how you speak, it's also about how you listen. Listen to what the interviewer has to say and engage with them positively. Do not come across as monotone, boring or disinterested. Always be positive!

Chapter 5
CSI Assessment Centre

*Important note: the following tests are of our own creation and are designed to help you prepare for the different assessments you may face. They are not designed to mimic the actual tests.

Following your telephone interview, you will face a short wait to find out whether you have been successful. If you are successful, then the next stage is an assessment centre. This essentially consists of a whole day of different exercises, finishing with a competency-based interview. The exercises that you will take can vary depending on the year in which you are taking the assessment, but may include:

• A numerical assessment;

• A verbal assessment, or written report exercise;

• A group exercise;

• An interview.

When the police inform you that you have been successful, they will also provide you with key information about the assessment day, including what exercises you'll have to take.

DID YOU KNOW?

A liquid fuel accelerant will generally leave behind a pool burn. This is a good way for investigators to tell whether a fire was started deliberately.

In this chapter, we will go through every single one of these potential assessments, and provide you with sample questions and answers to help you practise.

Preparing for the assessment centre

Prior to attending the assessment centre, it's imperative that you conduct a period of extensive preparation. Without preparing, it is extremely unlikely that you will pass the tests, as they are designed to separate the very best candidates from the crowd. This is particularly the case for the maths and literary-based assessments. In the maths tests, you will be scored on your accuracy and ability to perform moderately difficult calculations. In the literary assessments, you will be scored on elements such as grammar, spelling and punctuation. Maths in particular is difficult for many people, who may not have had much experience of utilising this since school. Therefore, you need to give yourself the best chance possible of passing, by practising as much as possible. Hopefully, this section should help you to do that! Along with using this book, we also recommend the following methods of preparing:

Purchase past practice maths and English papers online. Try and complete papers that are to a GCSE standard. This will undoubtedly improve your ability.

Learn the core competencies off by heart. This is especially important for the literary exercises and for the interview. The simple truth is that you won't pass the assessment centre if you can't demonstrate your understanding of the core competencies.

Start preparing early. Some people will only start

preparing for the assessment once they receive their test date confirmation, but this is a big mistake! You need to start preparing as soon as possible. Start preparing as soon as you've sent off your application form; because the more work you can do on it the better.

Practise interview techniques. This is something that not many people think to do, and ultimately lets them down. The more you practise your interview technique, the more familiar you will become with the process. This will make you relaxed during the interview, and come across better to the assessors.

Plan your journey. If you arrive late at the assessment centre, there is a good chance that you will not be accepted, and may have to start the application process all over again. Have all of your things in order the night before you attend, plan your route out so that you can arrive promptly and on time.

Now, let's look at the tests that you may need to take.

Numerical Assessment

First up, is the numerical assessment. This will consist of a series of maths based questions, ranging from simple calculations to data analysis and percentages. As we explained earlier, maths is really important for a crime scene investigator. Although you won't need to perform really complex maths, you will need to have a good concept of factors such as distance and measurements. The other reason that a numerical assessment helps to work out whether you will make a good crime scene investigator, is that it assesses your accuracy. There is no 'black and white' in maths, you are either wrong or you are right, and therefore accuracy is imperative.

The maths assessment will test you on:

- **Fractions and percentages.** For example, work out 10% of £432.

- **Data analysis.** You will be given a set of data and asked mathematical questions based on this data.

- **Decimals and rounding.** Questions requiring you to round up or down based on the decimal point.

- **Mean, mode and range.** You will be given a set of data and then asked to calculate various things.

- **Perimeter and area.** Here you'll have some shapes, and be asked to calculate measurements based on the shapes.

- **Angles.** You'll be given a shape, and asked to calculate the angles.

As you can see, this is all fairly rudimentary stuff. Along with all of this, there is also a possibility that you will be assessed on areas such as graphs, long division and algebra.

DID YOU KNOW?

If a CSI is required to photograph a (living) assault victim, they will often need to speak with the victim first, to gain their confidence and explain what they are doing. This makes interpersonal skills quite important for the role.

Now, it's time to practise your skills. Have a go at the practice assessment below, and then check your answers with those at the end of the test.

Practice Numerical Assessment

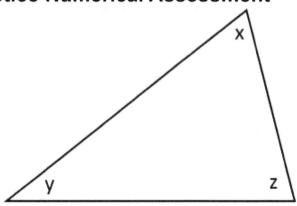

1. Below is a triangle.

(a) Using a protractor, calculate the angle *x*.

....

(1 mark)

(b) Using a protractor, calculate the angle *y*.

....

(1 mark)

(c) Using a protractor, calculate the angle *z*.

....

(1 mark)

(d) What mathematical term can be used to describe the type of triangle?

....

(1 mark)

2. (a) Write the following numbers in order of size, starting with the smallest.

0.3   30   0.03   0.31   30.1

....

(1 mark)

(b) Write the following numbers in order of size, starting with the biggest.

103   25   50   55   101

....

(1 mark)

(c) Write the following numbers in order of size, starting with the smallest.

25%   0.5   ⅕   75%   0.1

....

(1 mark)

3. (a) Convert 75% to its simplest fraction.

....

....

(2 marks)

(b) Work out which is the greater value:

60% of 950

Or

⅗ of 1,000

Explain your answer.

....

....

(2 marks)

4. Look at the shape below.

SCALE = 1cm x 1cm

Work out the perimeter.

....

(1 mark)

5. Here are five cards, each with its own number.

| 5 | 7 | 4 | 1 | 9 |

(a) The above number reads 57,419. Write this number in words.

....

....

....

(1 mark)

(i) Write the above number to the nearest **10**.

....

(1 mark)

(ii) Write the above number to the nearest **100**.

....

(1 mark)

(iii) Write the above number to the nearest **1,000**.

....

(1 mark)

6. Triangle ABC is a right angle.

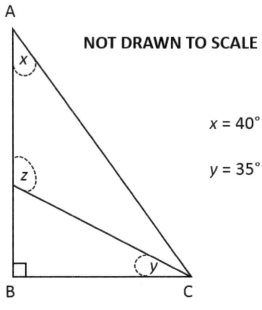

A

NOT DRAWN TO SCALE

x

$x = 40°$

$y = 35°$

z

y

B   C

Work out the angle of *z.*

....

....

....

Answer = ...

(2 marks)

7. Below shows four different companies with key information.

Company	Company Profit (Annual) (£)	Cost to buy company (£)	Number of employees
A	15,000	18,000	6
B	26,000	24,000	11
C	22,000	20,000	8
D	40,000	40,000	10

(a) How much profit did Company C make in the year?

....

Answer = ...

(1 mark)

(b) On average, how much did Company D make per month, based on the annual profit? To the nearest whole number.

....

....

Answer = ...

(1 mark)

(c) How much more did Company D make than Company B?

....

....

Answer = ...

(1 mark)

(d) If company A makes an increased profit of 8% in the following year, how much do they make in the following year?...

....

Answer = ...

(2 marks)

8. Study the following chart and answer the four questions that follow.

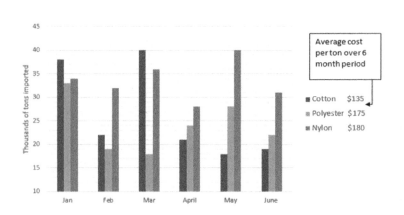

(a) What is the mean value for nylon imported over the 6 month period?

....

....

Answer = ...

(1 mark)

(b) What is the range for polyester imports across the 6 month period?

....

....

Answer = ...

(1 marks)

(c) What was the difference in thousands of tons between cotton material and nylon material imports across the first 3 months of the year?....................................

....

....

Answer = ...

(1 mark)

9. Jason is building a fence around his garden.

The diagram below shows the shape of Jason's garden with some of the measurements he is going to need.

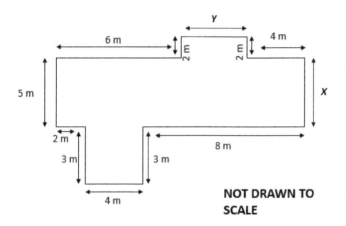

NOT DRAWN TO SCALE

Write down the measurements of **X** and **Y**.

X = ……………………………………………..

Y = ……………………………………………..

(2 marks)

10. Harrison, Katie and Ryan all work in a restaurant during their summer holidays.

In total, they earn £780 in tips in just 6 weeks.

They decide to split the money in the ratio of the number of hours each person worked. The ratio they split these tips into is 12 : 8 : 20.

Calculate how much each person will receive in tips.

....

....

....

....

Harrison = ...

Katie = ...

Ryan = ...

(2 marks)

Answers

1. (a) **68°**

    (b) **37°**

    (c) **75°**

    (d) **Scalene**

2. (a) **0.03,   0.3,   0.31,   30,   30.1**

Pay attention to where the decimal point is. It can be confusing because some of the numbers only have 2 numbers, whereas some have 3. You can always add a '0' to the end of the numbers, so that all of the decimals contain the same amount of numbers:

   0.03   0.30   0.31   30.0   30.1

   (b) **103,   101,   55,   50,   25**

Be sure to pay attention to what the question is asking you. This is a simple question, but it is asking you to write the numbers starting with the BIGGEST.

   (c) **0.1,   ⅕,   25%,   0.5,   75%**

Convert the numbers all into percentages to work out the order of size.

0.1 *= 10%*

⅕ *= 20%*

   25%

0.5 = 50%

75%

3. (a) ¾

75% as a fraction = 75 over 100 = $^{75}/_{100}$

Both of these numbers can be divided by 25 to simplify it to: ¾.

   (b) 3/5 of 1,000 is the greater value.

60% of 950 = 950 ÷ 100 = 9.5

9.5 x 60 = 570.

3/5 of 1000 = 1000 ÷ 5 = 200

200 x 3 = 600.

4. 22

You need to add up all of the sides of the outside of the shape. Remember the scale of the shape is 1cm by 1cm.

5. (a) fifty seven thousand four hundred and nineteen

The best way to write out the number is to read it out loud.

(b) (i) 57,420

To the nearest 10, the number 57,419 will be rounded up to 57,420.

The '9' in the units column determines what happens to the number in the tens column.

(b) (ii) 57,400

To the nearest 100, the number 57,419 will be rounded down to 57,400.

The number '1' in the tens column determines what happens to the number in the hundreds column.

(b) (iii) 57,000

To the nearest 1,000, the number 57,419 will be rounded down to 57,000.

The number '4' in the hundreds column determines what happens to the number in the thousands column.

6. (a) 125°

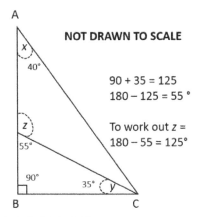

NOT DRAWN TO SCALE

90 + 35 = 125
180 − 125 = 55 °

To work out *z* =
180 − 55 = 125°

7. (a) £22,000

Company C made an annual profit of £22,000.

   (b) £3,333

40,000 ÷ 12 = 3333.333…

To the nearest whole number = £3333

   (c) £14,000

Company D = £40,000

Company B = £26,000

40,000 − 26,000 = 14,000

   (d) £16,200

15,000 ÷ 100 = 150

150 x 108 = 16,200

8. (a) 33.5

To work out the mean: add the totals up and divide by how many numbers there are:

34 + 32 + 36 + 28 + 40 + 31 = 201

201 ÷ 6 (months) = 33.5

(b) 15

To work out the range:

Highest polyester = 33

Lowest polyester = 18

33 – 18 = 15

(c) 2 thousand (of tons)

Cotton material in first 3 months:

38 + 22 + 40 = 100

Nylon material in first 3 months:

34 + 32 + 36 = 102

9. x = 5 m

y = 4 m

You need to use the side lengths already given to work out the side lengths missing.

For example, to work out side x, you know that this is parallel to the side to the left, and is the same height, therefore this must be the same as 5 m.

To work out side y, you know that the total width is 14 m
(2 + 4 + 8). So to work out side y, 14 – 6 – 4 = 4 m.

10.Harrison = £234

   Katie = £156

   Ryan = £390

   12 : 8 : 20 = 12 + 8 + 20 = 40

   £780 ÷ 40 = 19.5

   19.5 x 12 = £234 (Harrison)

   19.5 x 8 = £156 (Katie)

   19.5 x 20 = £390 (Ryan)

Data Analysis

Along with the above mathematical questions, there is also a good chance that you may need to sit some data analysis questions. Data analysis involves looking at sets of numbers and figures, and then answering questions based on these. Have a go at the questions below, and then compare your answers with ours.

QUESTION 1.

Kent Police have put out a tender for heating maintenance and installation. Below are quotes from 3 suppliers.

Heating maintenance and installation	**Supplier 1** Total cost over 3 years (£)	**Supplier 2** Total cost over 2 years (£)	**Supplier 3** Total cost over 5 years (£)
Installation and boiler replacements	24,630	19,750	36,150
Hot air systems	142,530	102,640	229,850
Service and maintenance	17,880	12,460	25,625

1. Amongst all three suppliers, based on an annual cost, what is the average cost to install hot air systems?

A. 45804

B. 50000

C. 48266

D. 47655

2. Based on 2 years, what supplier provides the most expensive quote for installation and boiler replacements?

A. Supplier 1

B. Supplier 2

C. Supplier 3

D. Supplier 1 and 3

3. What percentage of the total quote provided by Supplier 2 accounts for hot air systems?

A. 75%

B. 76.1%

C. 77.4%

D. 73.9%

QUESTION 2.

The Police Headquarters have put out a tender for security checks and system updates. Below are quotes from 3 suppliers.

Security checks and system updates	Supplier 1 Total cost over 2 years (£)	Supplier 2 Total cost over 4 years (£)	Supplier 3 Total cost over 5 years (£)
Basic Security Check	26,330	40,560	52,550
Advanced Security Check	52,530	104,320	120,880
Updating software and security	15,430	31,220	32,000

1. What percentage of the total quote provided by Supplier 2 accounts for updating software and security?

A. 12.4%

B. 17.7%

C. 19.2%

D. None of these

2. For the total cost over 5 years, what supplier provides the cheapest quote overall for security checks and system updates?

A. Supplier 1

B. Supplier 2

C. Supplier 3

D. Supplier 1 and 2

3. Based on an annual cost, what supplier provides the most expensive quote for basic security cost?

A. Supplier 1

B. Supplier 2

C. Supplier 3

D. All the same

QUESTION 3.

The Police Headquarters have put out a tender for fitness testing. Below are quotes from 3 suppliers.

Fitness Testing	Supplier 1 Total cost over 2 years (£)	Supplier 2 Total cost over 3 years (£)	Supplier 3 Total cost over 4 years (£)
Basic Fitness Training	9,800	10,500	16,650
Intense Fitness Training	19,000	23,500	34,500
8 week Fitness Programme	16,000	18,000	33,000

1. What percentage of the total quote provided by Supplier 2 accounts for intense fitness training?

A. 43.5%

B. 45.2%

C. 46%

D. 44.9%

2. Based on an annual one year cost, which supplier provides the most expensive overall quote for basic fitness training?

A. Supplier 1

B. Supplier 2

C. Supplier 3

D. Supplier 1 and 3

3. Based on an annual one year cost, which supplier provides the cheapest 8 week Fitness programme?

A. Supplier 1

B. Supplier 2

C. Supplier 3

D. All the same

QUESTION 4.

Kent Police have put out a tender for uniform dry cleaning and alterations. Below are quotes from 3 suppliers.

Uniform dry cleaning and amendments	**Supplier 1** Total cost over 1 years (£)	**Supplier 2** Total cost over 3 years (£)	**Supplier 3** Total cost over 2 years (£)
Dry cleaning	9,600	26,700	19,020
Alterations	5,500	14,900	11,000
Cleaning and alterations - Full package	13,450	38,850	25,800

1. Based on an annual one year cost, which supplier provides the cheapest dry cleaning services?

A. Supplier 1

B. Supplier 2

C. Supplier 3

D. All the same

2. For the total cost over 3 years, what supplier provides the cheapest quote overall for cleaning and alterations – full package?

A. Supplier 1

B. Supplier 2

C. Supplier 3

D. All the same

3. Based on an annual cost and everything the supplier has to offer, what supplier is the most expensive?

A. Supplier 1

B. Supplier 2

C. Supplier 3

D. All the same

QUESTION 5.

Kent Police have put out a tender for electrical equipment and supplies. Below are quotes from 3 suppliers.

Electrical Equipment and supplies	**Supplier 1** Total cost over 2 years (£)	**Supplier 2** Total cost over 2 years (£)	**Supplier 3** Total cost over 1 years (£)
Basic Services	34,550	36,660	15,450
Electrical and safety check	39,550	42,000	20,000
Full equipment maintenance	120,850	150,500	60,000

1. Based on an annual year cost, which supplier offers the best price for electrical safety checks?

A. Supplier 1

B. Supplier 2

C. Supplier 3

D. They are the same

2. What percentage of the total quote provided by supplier 1 accounts for basic services?

A. 17%

B. 17.7%

C. 18.5%

D. 18.3%

3. Based on 2 years, what supplier provides the cheapest quote overall for electrical equipment and supplies?

A. Supplier 1

B. Supplier 2

C. Supplier 3

D. Supplier 2 and 3

Answers

Question 1

1. Amongst all three suppliers, based on an annual cost, what is the average cost to install hot air systems?

Answer - 48266

2. Based on 2 years, what supplier provides the most expensive quote for installation and boiler replacements?

Answer - Supplier 2

3. What percentage of the total quote provided by Supplier 2 accounts for hot air systems?

Answer - 76.1%

Question 2

1. What percentage of the total quote provided by Supplier 2 accounts for updating software and security?

Answer - 17.7%

2. For the total cost over 5 years, what supplier provides the cheapest quote overall for security checks and system updates?

Answer - Supplier 3

3. Based on an annual cost, what supplier provides the most expensive quote for installation and boiler replacements?

Answer – Supplier 1

Question 3

1. What percentage of the total quote provided by Supplier 2 accounts for intense fitness training?

Answer – 45.2%

2. Based on an annual one year cost, which supplier provides the most expensive overall quote for basic fitness training?

Answer – Supplier 1

3. Based on an annual one year cost, which supplier provides the cheapest 8 week Fitness programme?

Answer – Supplier 2

Question 4

1. Based on an annual one year cost, which supplier provides the cheapest dry cleaning services?

Answer – Supplier 2

2. For the total cost over 3 years, what supplier provides the cheapest quote overall for cleaning and alterations – full package?

Answer – Supplier 3

3. Based on an annual cost and everything the supplier

has to offer, what supplier is the most expensive?

Answer – Supplier 1

Question 5

1. Based on an annual year cost, which supplier offers the best price for electrical safety checks?

Answer - Supplier 1

2. What percentage of the total quote provided by supplier 1 accounts for basic services?

Answer - 17.7%

3. Based on 2 years, what supplier provides the cheapest quote overall for electrical equipment and supplies?

Answer - Supplier 3

Literacy Assessment

Next, you will be required to undertake a literacy based assessment. There are two ways in which you could be tested here, and they are as follows:

- You might be asked to sit a verbal reasoning exercise, which assesses your attention to detail.

- You might be asked to take a written report exercise, which will assess your grammar, spelling and punctuation, as well as the quality of your written communication.

Literacy skills are extremely important for crime scene investigators. You must be able to compile in-depth and accurate reports based on your findings at a crime scene. These reports need to be good enough that they can be used in court, and further on in the investigation. Remember that accuracy and communication are both core competencies of a CSI, and this assessment will test both of these areas. The written report exercise will also test your attention to detail. Let's have a look at a sample question from this exercise:

Written Report, Sample Question

During the written report exercise, you will be given a page containing information on a crime scene. It is your job to separate the essential facts from the useless facts, and then construct this into a written report. The information on the page will be deliberately messy and unorganised, it will mix up details and provide you with evidence or information that isn't particularly relevant to the case. You need to pick out the **important** details, and then assemble them into a short report. You will also be expected to point out any inaccuracies in the report. For example, if the report contradicts itself on details such as hair colour, murder weapon, etc. Let's take a look at an example:

Case Report

At 5pm on January 6th a woman was found dead. The weather outside was very cold and the woman had short brown hair. She lived on Ficshire Road, in Norfolk. The day she was found was Tuesday, but she went to meet with a friend on Friday 1st of January. The woman's name was Janet. Analysis of blood taken from the flat showed that Janet had fought with her attacker before she died. She was married to a man named Tim Gordon, and had taken his last name in marriage. There appeared to be signs of a struggle. The woman was found inside her flat, number 2 Ficshire Road. Her husband was nowhere to be seen. Janet was found by her sister, who had a spare key to the flat. She had been stabbed multiple times with a knife that was found in the toilet cistern, but had been taken from her kitchen drawer. There was blood in the sink and blood on the kitchen wall. There was a pool of blood by the kitchen door. A table was on its side and there was cutlery and broken plates all over the floor. Janet turned 43 years old on Saturday 3rd January. Investigators determined that she was murdered 2 days before she was discovered. She worked for a printing company called *PrintHappy* and had been there for 4 years prior to her death. Janet's body was found in a defensive position. Investigators found a shopping list on the kitchen counter that indicated she had eaten chicken soup for dinner on Friday. Her son is called Nathan. There was a large, visible fingerprint on the kitchen window that did not belong to Janet. Janet loved to go clothes shopping and had a very expensive collection of clothing. In particular, she loved her red boots from *Smart Shoes*. Janet's phone was a Nokia. It was blue, and had a cover containing a picture of a seal. Janet's friend Pamela was seen visiting her on Sunday. Pamela has a daughter called Michelle. Janet did not call in sick on Monday, or on Tuesday, but didn't attend work either. A neighbour reported hearing a loud bang from inside Janet's flat, on Saturday morning. The same neighbour bumped into Janet at the supermarket, on Saturday afternoon. Janet was buying asparagus, for her dinner. At 6pm on Sunday, a call was placed from Janet's mobile phone to her mother, but she hung up without saying anything. When her mother tried to call her back, there was no answer. Janet's phone was discovered in the toilet, where someone had apparently tried to flush it. Her son Nathan works at a fast food restaurant.

How To Break This Down

Obviously, there is an enormous amount of information here. So, how do you break it down? The first thing you need to do is to read through the entire paragraph carefully. As you do this, you should already start picking up on things that are relevant/irrelevant. Draw a table, and then separate the information into columns. Alternatively, you could simply highlight all of the relevant information in the passage, as you go through. We've done this below, to help you:

At 5pm on January 6th a woman was found dead. The weather outside was very cold and the woman had short brown hair. She lived on **Ficshire Road, in Norfolk**. **The day she was found was Tuesday**, but she went to meet with a friend on Friday 1st of January. **The woman's name was Janet**. **Analysis of blood taken from the flat showed that Janet had fought with her attacker before she died.** She was **married to a man named Tim Gordon,** and had taken his last name in marriage. **There appeared to be signs of a struggle**. The woman was found inside her flat, number 2 Ficshire Road. **Her**

husband was nowhere to be seen. Janet was found by her sister, who had a spare key to the flat. She had been stabbed multiple times with a knife that was found in the toilet cistern, but had been taken from her kitchen drawer. There was blood in the sink and blood on the kitchen wall. There was a pool of blood by the kitchen door. A table was on its side and there was cutlery and broken plates all over the floor. Janet turned 43 years old on Saturday 3rd January. Investigators determined that **she was murdered 2 days before she was discovered.** She worked for a printing company called *PrintHappy* and had been there for 4 years prior to her death. **Janet's body was found in a defensive position.** Investigators found a shopping list on the kitchen counter that indicated she had eaten chicken soup for dinner on Friday. Her son is called Nathan. **There was a large, visible fingerprint on the kitchen window that did not belong to Janet.** Janet loved to go clothes shopping and had a very expensive collection of clothing. In particular, she loved her red boots from *Smart Shoes*. Janet's phone was a Nokia. It was blue, and had a cover containing a picture of a seal. **Janet's friend Pamela was seen visiting her on Sunday.** Pamela has a daughter called Michelle. **Janet did not call in sick on Monday, or on Tuesday, but didn't attend work either.** A neighbour reported hearing a loud bang from inside Janet's flat, on Saturday morning. The same neighbour bumped into Janet at the supermarket, on Saturday afternoon. Janet was buying asparagus, for her dinner. **At 6pm on Sunday, a call was placed from Janet's mobile phone to her mother, but she hung up without saying anything.**

When her mother tried to call her back, there was no answer. Janet's phone was discovered in the toilet, where someone had apparently tried to flush it. Her son Nathan works at a fast food restaurant.

So, using the above information, we can glean the following:

• A woman named Janet Gordon was found dead in her flat, at 5pm on Sunday 6th January.

• She was discovered by her sister, who had a spare key to the flat.

• Janet lived at number 2 Ficshire Road, Norfolk.

• Janet was married to a man named Tim, who has not been contactable since the murder.

• Janet's body was found in a defensive position.

• Janet had been stabbed on multiple occasions. There was blood in the sink, blood on the kitchen wall, and a pool of blood by the kitchen door. Analysis of blood taken from the flat showed that Janet had fought with her attacker before she died.

• The murder weapon was a knife that had been taken from Janet's kitchen drawer, and then left in the toilet cistern by the killer.

• The flat was extremely messy, with a table overturned and cutlery and broken plates on the floor.

• There was an unknown fingerprint on the window. This fingerprint did not belong to Janet.

- Investigators have determined that Janet was murdered on Sunday, two days before she was discovered.

- On Sunday, Janet's friend Pamela was seen visiting her.

- Janet did not call in sick to work on Monday or Tuesday, but didn't attend work either.

- At 6pm on Sunday evening, a call was placed from Janet's mobile to her mother, but the caller hung up without speaking. When Janet's mother tried to call back, there was no answer.

- Somebody had attempted to flush Janet's phone down the toilet.

- Janet's husband is missing.

You will also notice that we have underlined a sentence in the passage. This is because this line contradicts other information that is given in the passage. Janet was found on Tuesday 6th January, and turned 43 years old on Saturday 3rd January. Therefore, the passage is incorrect in stating that she met with a friend on Friday 1st January, this could not be the correct date. You will be expected to notice this, and point it out.

Now, you need to take the information above and turn it into an accurate and logical report. Below we've given you an example of how this can be done:

At 5pm on Tuesday 6th January, Janet Gordon was found dead in her flat – number 2, Ficshire Road.

Mrs. Gordon was discovered by her sister, who had a spare key to the flat. Mrs. Gordon had been stabbed on multiple occasions, with a knife that had been taken from her kitchen drawer, and then left in the toilet cistern. This indicates that someone had attempted to hide the weapon. There was blood in the sink, blood on the kitchen wall and a pool of blood by the kitchen door. Analysis of blood showed that Janet had fought with her attacker before she was killed, and her body was found in a defensive position. To add to this, the flat was extremely messy, with a table overturned and objects such as cutlery and broken plates on the floor. Investigators discovered an unknown fingerprint on the window, which did not belong to Janet. They have determined that Janet died two days before she was discovered, meaning that she was killed on Sunday 4th January. On Sunday 4th January, Janet's friend Pamela was seen visiting her. To add to this, on Sunday evening, a call was placed from Janet's phone to her mother's mobile. When Janet's mother answered, there was no response, and the caller immediately hung up. Upon ringing Janet back, her mother received no response. Janet's mobile phone was later discovered in the toilet, where someone had tried to flush it. Naturally, given that Janet was killed on Sunday, she did not attend work on Monday or Tuesday, nor did she call in sick. As of yet, Janet's husband Gordon has not been contactable.

It is my recommendation that the fingerprint on the window be crosschecked against the knife found in the toilet system, for matching prints. The primary lead in the case should be Janet's friend Pamela. The police should also give immediate priority to finding Janet's husband, Gordon.

Finally, I would like to point out that there is a discrepancy in the official report. The report states that Janet met with her friend on Friday 1st January. This is incorrect, as Janet's birthday was on Saturday 3rd January, and she was discovered on Tuesday 6th January.

As you can see, we have constructed a report here that is grammatically correct, precise, and covers all of the essential/relevant details of the case. We have laid out all of the important facts in logical order, and taken the initiative to suggest further investigation measures, and our opinion on some of the details – such as hidden objects.

Below we've provided you with some more sample passages, to give you practice at this exercise. Before you start though, here are some top tips:

- Pay attention to grammar, punctuation and spelling. You will be marked down if your report contains grammatical mistakes. It's essential that you are as accurate and clear as possible.

- Structure your report. You can clearly see in our report how we have laid out the details in a logical order – starting with the discovery of the body and the crime scene, before moving on to our recommendations and observations.

- Think really carefully about the information that has been presented to you. Some of the information is deliberately placed, to try and trip you up. For example, our sample passage makes reference to a 'large bang heard on Saturday morning'. This might sound important, but in the grand scheme of the investigation, it's not. Janet was seen alive on Saturday afternoon, and on Sunday was being visited by her friend.

- Layout your report like a letter. Don't just throw all of the facts down. You can see in our report that it's almost as if we have addressed it to someone.

Now, have a go at the following sample reports. We've left you with two extra pages for each answer. Use the first page to plan your response, and the second to write your report.

Sample Report Writing: Question 1

Read the following passage, and then construct a crime scene report based on the evidence.

Nathan Gunn was 24 years old. He was found dead in his car on Ficshire Lane, at 03:30am. A passer-by noticed that the car had been parked in the same place for several days, and went to take a look. Nathan had short brown hair and a stud in his left ear. The stud was made of diamond, and had been purchased from a jewellery store named *Chains' N Things.* Nathan had been shot once in the head. The exit wound indicated that he had been shot from the right hand side. He was in the passenger seat of the car, slumped against the door. Investigators noted that his hands were in a relaxed position, indicating that he did not expect the gunshot. Nathan's mother is 65 years old, and works at a local clothing store. Her managers, Daryl and Jay, claim that she is an extremely hard worker and one of their best staff members. Nathan was known to police as a drug dealer. In the boot of his car, they found a briefcase, containing a substantial quantity of various class A drugs. Along with this, they discovered a VHS tape. When played back, this showed a recording of Nathan speaking in violent terms about a man named Josh. Nathan had a substantial criminal record, and had been questioned only last week regarding a burglary on Ficshire Road. Nathan was also a keen table-tennis player. There was a significant amount of blood on both the passenger and driver seats of the car, and on the gearbox. Smear patterns on the seat indicated that Nathan had not died in the passenger seat, and had been dragged over to this position. The driver's side window was rolled down. Nathan's brother Mark works in a local bakery. The bakery is located on Ficshire Road. Mark claims that on the night Nathan was killed, he saw Nathan's friend Peter get into his car. CCTV train station footage near the scene picked up Peter running away, at half past 1 in the morning, on the 1st June. Investigation of the body indicated that Nathan was killed at approximately the same time. Police have been unable to locate Peter since the incident. Nathan previously went to school at Ficshire Preparatory. Many of his old school friends have expressed devastation at his death, and offered their condolences. This included his ex-girlfriend Peggy. The murder weapon was found hidden in a bin near to the scene.

Planning Page

Sample Response

Sample Report Writing: Question 2

Read the following passage, and then construct a crime scene report based on the evidence.

At 2pm on Monday 3rd July, a burglary took place. The burglary was committed on a house in Ficshire Lane, owned by Sarah Dean. Sarah placed a phone call at 2pm, informing the police that she had arrived home from the shops, to discover two men inside her house. Upon seeing Sarah, the men fled. Sarah works at the local pet store, where she helps cats and dogs to find new homes. Upon arriving back home, Sarah discovered that her kitchen window had been smashed and then forced open. There was a bootprint on the kitchen counter, and a substantial amount of mud on the floor. Sarah claims that the mud was not there when she left the house to go shopping. Sarah has blonde hair, green eyes and is approximately 5 foot 4 in height. Her favourite food is jelly, and there were substantial amounts of this in her fridge at the time of the burglary. Sarah claims that the thieves stole an extremely expensive ring from her bedside cupboard, and also stole an expensive leather jacket from her wardrobe. The leather jacket was genuine lambskin, and cost in excess of £2000. In their rush to leave the building, the thieves left behind a small hammer. The hammer was found near a locked cupboard door, which contained a number of dents in it. Investigators have surmised that the thieves were trying to break into the cupboard, but were disturbed when Sarah arrived home. Upon further investigation of the property, investigators discovered a pair of woman's wellington boots hidden in the garden shed. The mud on the bottom of the boots matched with that found in the kitchen, and with the footprint on the kitchen counter. Sarah's brother, Michael, is a well-known drug addict. Police arrested him last week on suspicion of selling stolen goods. Sarah has informed police that she intends to claim on the insurance for the stolen goods, and is devastated by the loss of her leather jacket. Sarah had the day off from work on Monday, as she was suffering from the flu.

Planning Page

Sample Response

Verbal Reasoning Test

Alternatively, you might be given a different type of literary assessment, again testing the strength of your observational skills.

In this assessment, you will be given a short paragraph, containing some information about an event or case. You will need to read through the paragraph and then decide whether the statements following it are TRUE, FALSE or IMPOSSIBLE TO SAY.

When you do this exercise, it is extremely important that you base your answers ONLY on what is given in the paragraph. You must not respond to the question based on your own opinions or views.

Sample Question

A fire has occurred in a nightclub belonging to Harry James. One person died in the fire, which occurred at 11pm on Saturday night. The club was insured for less than its value.

QUESTIONS – TRUE, FALSE OR IMPOSSIBLE TO SAY?

1. The fire occurred at 1100 hours.

2. A relative of Harry James was killed in the fire.

3. If the insurance company decide to pay out for the fire, Harry James stands to make a profit.

4. The fire was caused by arson.

5. The club was insured at the time of the fire.

How To Answer

Q1. The passage states that the fire occurred at 11pm – which is 2300 hours military time. Therefore, the answer is **FALSE.**

Q2. The passage only states that one person died, and not who they were or their relation to Harry James. We cannot know if the person who died was related to Harry. Therefore, the answer is **IMPOSSIBLE TO SAY.**

Q3. The passage states that the club was insured for less than its value, meaning Harry won't make a profit. Therefore, the answer is **FALSE.**

Q4. The passage does not mention how the fire started/what it was caused by. Therefore, the answer is **IMPOSSIBLE TO SAY.**

Q5. The passage states that the club was insured for less than its value. Therefore, the answer is **TRUE.**

Now, have a go at the following questions, in the same style.

Sample Verbal Reasoning Test

Question 1

An accident occurred on the M6 motorway between junctions 8 and 9 southbound at 3pm. The driver of a Ford Fiesta was seen to pull into the middle lane without indicating, forcing another car to veer into the central reservation. One person suffered a broken arm and was taken to hospital before the police arrived.

QUESTIONS – TRUE, FALSE OR IMPOSSIBLE TO SAY?

1. The accident was on the M6 motorway on the carriageway that leads to Scotland.

2. The driver of the Ford Fiesta was injured in the crash.

3. The central reservation was responsible for the accident.

4. The police did not give first aid at the scene.

5. The accident happened at 1500 hours.

Question 2

A man of between 30 and 35 years of age was seen stealing a car from outside Mrs Brown's house yesterday. He was seen breaking the nearside rear window with a hammer before driving off at 40 miles per hour. He narrowly missed a young mother who was pushing a pram.

QUESTIONS – TRUE, FALSE OR IMPOSSIBLE TO SAY?

1. The man who stole the car was 34 years old.

2. He stole Mrs Brown's car.

3. The young mother who was pushing a pram was injured.

4. He used a hammer to smash the windscreen.

5. When he drove off he was breaking the speed limit.

Question 3

A shopkeeper called Mr Smith was seen serving alcohol to a girl aged 16.

The girl had shown him fake ID, which was a driving licence belonging to her sister. The incident occurred at around 11.30pm on a Wednesday evening during December.

QUESTIONS – TRUE, FALSE OR IMPOSSIBLE TO SAY?

1. The girl is old enough to purchase alcohol from Mr Smith.

2. The girl purchased the alcohol for her sister.

3. The girl's sister had given the driving licence to her.

4. Mr Smith will receive a custodial sentence for his actions.

Question 4

Following a bank robbery in a town centre, 6 masked gunmen were seen speeding away from the scene in a black van. The incident, which happened in broad daylight in front of hundreds of shoppers, was picked up by CCTV footage.

Police are appealing for witnesses. The local newspaper has offered a £5,000 reward for any information leading to the conviction of all the people involved.

QUESTIONS – TRUE, FALSE OR IMPOSSIBLE TO SAY?

1. The car in which the gunmen drove off was a black van.

2. Someone must have seen something.

3. The incident was picked up by CCTV cameras.

4. The newspaper will pay £5,000 for information leading to the arrest of all of the men involved.

5. Police are not appealing to members of the public for help.

Question 5

A factory fire at 'Stevenage Supplies' was arson, the police have confirmed. A man was seen running away from the scene shortly before the fire started. Earlier that day a man was sacked from the company for allegedly stealing money from the safe. The incident is the second one to occur at the factory in as many months.

QUESTIONS – TRUE, FALSE OR IMPOSSIBLE TO SAY?

1. Police have confirmed that the fire at the factory was arson.

2. The man who was seen running away from the fire was the man who started it.

3. One previous 'fire-related' incident has already occurred at the factory.

4. The man who was sacked from the factory may have started the fire.

Question 6

At 1800 hours today, police issued a statement in relation to the crime scene in Armstrong Road. Police have been examining the scene all day and reports suggest that it may be murder. Forensic officers have been visiting the incident and inform us that the whole street has been cordoned off and nobody will be allowed through. Police say that the street involved will be closed for another 18 hours and no access will be available to anyone during this time.

QUESTIONS – TRUE, FALSE OR IMPOSSIBLE TO SAY?

1. Police have confirmed the incident is murder.

2. Forensic officers have now left the scene.

3. The road will be open at 12 noon the following day.

4. Although the street has been cordoned off, taxis and buses will be given access.

5. Forensic officers will be at the scene all night.

Question 7

Mrs Rogers telephoned the police at 8pm to report a burglary at her house in Gamble Crescent. She reports that she came home from work and her front bedroom window was open but she doesn't remember leaving it open. She informs the police that her jewellery box is missing and also £40 cash, which was left on the kitchen table. She came home from work at 5pm and left again at 7am in the morning. No other signs of forced entry were visible.

QUESTIONS – TRUE, FALSE OR IMPOSSIBLE TO SAY?

1. The burglar made his/her way in through the bedroom window.

2. The burglar took the jewellery and £40 cash before leaving.

3. Mrs Rogers was away from the house for 10 hours in total.

4. Mrs Rogers may have left the window open herself before leaving for work.

5. There were other visible signs of forced entry.

Question 8

The local bank was held up at gunpoint on Monday the 18th of September at approximately 4pm. The thieves used a black motorcycle to make their getaway. The following facts are also known about the incident:

• *Two shots were fired.*

• *There were 12 staff members on duty at the time of the raid.*

• *The alarm was raised by the manager and the police were called.*

• *The cashier was ordered to hand over a bag of money containing £7,000.*

• *The thieves have not yet been caught.*

• *Police are appealing for witnesses.*

QUESTIONS – TRUE, FALSE OR IMPOSSIBLE TO SAY?

1. The thieves have been caught.

2. The cashier raised the alarm.

3. The cashier was shot.

4. Two people were injured.

5. The bank was open for business at the time of the incident.

Question 9

A father and son were found dead in their two-bedroom flat in Sparsbrook on Sunday evening. They had both been suffocated. The following facts are also known:

• *The victims were identified by the police as Mark Webster, 16 years old, and his father, Thomas Webster, 39 years old.*

• *Thomas was in debt to the sum of £37,000.*

• *Two men were seen leaving the house at 4pm on Sunday afternoon.*

• *Two men were seen acting suspiciously in the area on Saturday evening before driving off in a Brown Ford Escort car.*

• *Thomas had previously contacted the police to express his concerns about his safety following threats from his creditors.*

• *The house had not been broken into.*

QUESTIONS – TRUE, FALSE OR IMPOSSIBLE TO SAY?

1. The people Thomas owed money to could have been responsible for the deaths.

2. The two men seen leaving the house were not responsible for the deaths of Mark Webster and Thomas Webster.

3. The house had been broken into.

4. Neighbours reported two men acting suspiciously in the area on Saturday evening.

5. The people responsible for the deaths drove off in a brown Ford Escort car.

Question 10

Firefighters have discovered a large quantity of cannabis during a fire on a farm in the village of Teynsville. Police have cordoned off the area. The following facts are also known about the incident:

• *The farm is owned by local farmer Peter Watts.*

• *The fire was deliberately started.*

• *Peter Watts has two previous convictions for possession and supply of Class A drugs.*

• *Peter Watts's wife was at home on the night of the fire.*

• *Peter Watts was visiting friends in the nearby town of Grentshill when the fire started.*

• *A passer-by reported the fire to the police at 9pm.*

• *Peter Watts has been arrested on suspicion of possession of cannabis.*

QUESTIONS – TRUE, FALSE OR IMPOSSIBLE TO SAY?

1. Cannabis is a Class A drug.

2. The fire was started accidentally.

3. A passer-by reported the fire to the fire service at 9pm.

4. The cannabis found during the fire belonged to Peter Watts.

5. Peter Watts has been arrested for possession of cannabis.

Answers:

Question 1

1. Impossible to say

2. Impossible to say

3. False

4. True

5. True

Question 2

1. Impossible to say

2. Impossible to say

3. False

4. False

5. Impossible to say

Question 3

1. False

2. Impossible to say

3. Impossible to say

4. Impossible to say

Question 4

1. True

2. Impossible to say

3. True

4. False

5. False

Question 5

1. True

2. Impossible to say

3. True

4. True

Question 6

1. False

2. Impossible to say

3. True

4. False

5. Impossible to say

Question 7

1. Impossible to say

2. Impossible to say

3. False

4. True

5. False

Question 8

1. False

2. False

3. Impossible to say

4. Impossible to say

5. Impossible to say

Question 9

1. True

2. Impossible to say

3. False

4. Impossible to say

5. Impossible to say

Question 10

1. Impossible to say

2. False

3. False

4. Impossible to say

5. False

Group Exercise

Next up, you might be required to take part in a group exercise. This exercise is designed to test a number of attributes, but in particular, it will assess you on your communication and teamwork skills. As we have mentioned, crime scene investigators must have great communication skills. This is particularly important when it comes to communicating with new people. On many occasions, you will be acting as a 'lone wolf' from your constabulary at crime scenes, and will need to communicate and work with people whom you have never met before. Therefore, this exercise is a great test of how well you can do this. For this exercise, you'll be placed in a room with a number of people whom you will never have met, and you will need to work as a group to come to a solution to the problem you have been given.

Group activities consider more than straight communication, they reveal:

• The dynamics that go on between people and how you react;

• How you deal with conflict;

• Whether you can instigate ideas;

• How obstructive you might be;

• How you respond to the ideas of others;

• Whether you are a leader or follower;

• The extent to which you are able to build on other ideas;

• The amount to which you are compliant and willing to go with the group.

These activities are therefore there to test or assess how you react in people-focused situations and to put you under some form of pressure. We can all be on our best behaviour while the world is ordered and things are going well, but very often we revert to type under pressure. It is when we are under pressure that we see how short a person's temper really is, or how they handle discord in the group. Of course all this is not happening in isolation because you also need to perform within the group and solve a puzzle or situation, which again takes your eye off the ball and distracts you from concentrating on how you want to portray your behaviour.

When you take part in a group activity it is very likely that the observers will already have your psychometric assessment and will be looking at behaviour that either refutes or endorses what it says, and therefore group activities are a way of double-checking your skills and behaviour.

When you are asked to undertake a group activity you

will be given a scenario and you may also be given roles – not quite, "You are Professor Green in the library," – more like, "You are the HR manager," – but you get the picture. You are expected to conduct the meeting or take part in the activity in the role of that person and represent whatever company your role play asks of you. If you are given a role, then be assured that everyone else will be too. You may also be given additional papers to read through.

You will then be asked to enter a room where you will enact the activity (there may be a table and chairs) and several chairs with their backs against the walls. The chairs against the wall, facing inwards, are for your observers, and they may even be sitting there when you enter the room. These observers are the assessors for this activity. They will be watching you intently throughout the activity and will mark significant facts regarding your comments, body language and behaviour on sheets of paper throughout the activity. The observers will not speak to you throughout the entire activity and often remain in the room even after you have left. You may find that they do not even make eye contact with you; they endeavour to stay as neutral as possible.

Enact the activity as you would in real life. You will find that as you progress, you will be drawn into the activity and this is where your real behaviour is shown, but it is best to try to remember that you are being assessed at all times.

Tip: try to read the competency list before going into a group activity. These are the behaviours

the observers will be looking for and marking you against.

After a set period of time, perhaps an hour, the activity will be stopped whether you have made the decision, solved the problem or finished the meeting. The objective from the observer's point of view is to see you in action and they will have seen plenty of you in an hour! At this point you will probably be asked to leave the room to have a break, while the assessors retire to write up their notes and confer.

Put very briefly then, the process is:

1. You may be given information or a role (if so read thoroughly).

2. You will be asked to enter the room and sit down.

3. You will be observed undertaking a group activity and marked on your language, body language, content and style.

4. You will be stopped after a set amount of time.

5. You will leave the room.

What types of group activity are there?

A group activity can be any activity that includes a number of people. However they mainly take the form of:

Team meetings

These aim to replicate a typical team meeting. If this

is chosen, then you will be given an agenda and some notes. You will also need to know what type of team it is and whether there are any issues that need addressing within the meeting.

Important point: this is your team. The assessors will be looking for a team or collaborative approach and therefore you will not receive favour for flaring up or setting yourself (or other team members) against one another or the rest of the team. The days of ruling by fear are long gone in most industries. Also, if you have been given an issue to address (such as excessive sickness), make sure you do and don't skirt around the issue or run out of time.

If you are truly going to manage a team and deliver on your business targets through and with these people they need to look up to you and see leadership at the most and mutual respect at the least. This MUST be exhibited through every part of your communication and that means your actions (even when you think no one is looking). Therefore totally rule out any rolling of the eyes, sarcastic looks, laughing at others contributions, or staring out of the window.

OR

Problem solving groups

This form of group activity will present you with a problem that you are expected to solve. The big mistake that most people make here is that they concentrate on solving the problem – well that is hardly surprising as that is what you are here for isn't it?

Actaully, no. If you solve the problem in the allotted time, well and good, but actually you are being assessed on your behavioural skills too. In fact quite often the problem is one that cannot easily be solved and therefore the most you can do is make headway with the group.

Although it is important to work on the problem, what you are being judged on is just HOW you do that.

DID YOU KNOW?

When investigating a murder, the victim's hands, feet and head are covered in plastic bags, to prevent debris evidence from leaving the body.

How To Approach The Exercise

After the general introductions, see if anyone would like to chair the meeting and suggest an appropriate process or structure for the task. If no one comes forward, then suggest yourself.

You need to start off by looking at the problem. Why is it a problem? For whom? What impact does this have on the business? Find out how it impacts on each person and their business area by asking everyone to comment on where they see issues with the problem from their own business perspective.

Explore where there are unknowns and assumptions (because this is likely to be a role play exercise) and put those up on a flip chart if possible. Get everyone to contribute towards possible solutions and if you are the chair, steer the discussion. However, if you are not the chair you will need to demonstrate your realms of influence by suggesting a structure or way forward for the meeting.

Therefore:

1. The race is not on to find the quickest solution;

2. You must involve everyone in the discussions;

3. Work out first how you are going to work together as a group;

4. Make a joint plan as to how you use your time in the group (AND the process you will go through);

5. Ensure everyone has a fair chance to speak;

6. Note up on a flip chart (if there is one) everyone's ideas (and explore whether there are areas where you lack information or knowledge);

7. Don't worry if you do not get as far as solving the problem by the end of the meeting.

Debating

Holding a debating group activity adds a little extra to the mix. Not only are you demonstrating how you work with others and in a group, but you are also demonstrating your values and thought processes. It is almost impossible to debate a subject without giving a lot of yourself away. This can be a good thing or not – depending on your views. For example, if you were to go to an assessment centre at a pharmaceutical company you may be faced with debating 'Should animals be used for pharmaceutical testing?'

Consider for one moment how you stand on this (highly emotive) subject. It would be impossible to debate this subject without revealing your core values and principles, and the debating itself may get you rather hot under the collar, whichever side of the debate you are on.

Consider also if you were asked to uphold the debate for the other side of the argument. What would you say? Would you be able to deliver? Perhaps you would find that one step too far? Of course, only you can decide, but you will be judged on your response.

Debates are often thought of in terms of polar opposites but there is usually some common ground that both sides can agree on, and this should be explored and noted. We all have differing views about life's issues and you need not to appear as if an open discussion quickly becomes open combat! Neither is it OK to just have one dogged view, in a debating exercise you must be able to substantiate that view.

Therefore:

1. Think about your values – how do you really feel about this subject?

2. If you are asked to hold a view that is not your own, consider first how this makes you feel. If you can live with it, then go with it.

3. Just because it is a debate does not mean that it is an argument. It needs a structure.

4. Start by asking everyone to share their views.

5. Decide as a group how you are going to include everyone's ideas.

6. Work together to elicit areas of common agreement.

7. Remember you are still being observed – the debate is only the vehicle for a discussion. IT IS STILL A TEAM ACTIVITY.

Negotiating

Negotiating is a high-level skill and it takes any form of debating one step higher. A debate may centre on you holding your view but in a negotiation the emphasis is on persuading and influencing the other person to accept your view. For this to happen, finding that common ground on which you can agree can become even more important, for if we can find an area of agreement we can explore our difference from that point.

All managers need to negotiate and in essence all of us need to be able to undertake this skill in varying areas of our lives. For example, have you ever wanted to negotiate on the price of a car? A new house? Some furniture? Your future salary? All of these are real life situations where we need to negotiate. Doing so in a group activity is simply taking that one step further. A word to the wise: if you are thinking of annihilating your opponent here, you need to think again. You may walk away the winner but that approach is not good for long term business. The other party will feel small and insignificant and will not want to do business with you again. This approach is often called **I win:you lose** and it is not a good outcome in business.

Let's look at the other possible outcomes:

I lose:you win – This is great for you as you may now feel on top of the world, feeling that you have won over me, but it is not long until I start feeling resentful. Whether I blame you for winning or myself for being weak and ill-prepared, I do not feel like I want to meet with you again. I may even feel that the power ratio between us has shifted in your favour. All in all, once again not a helpful way to continue in business and a situation I would rather forget than be reminded of – and therefore I would not be seeking you out in the future (and I am sure your observer will not think well of you losing to a competitor outright – it does not bode well for the business).

I lose:you lose – Oh dear, what happened here? In this position we both lost. Perhaps neither of us negotiated a good deal, or we failed to reach a settlement – leaving us both feeling frustrated and dissatisfied. On a positive note, if we recognise the situation in time we could adjourn or re-think our approach – possibly setting another date in the near future to come together again but any assessor observing you here would score you a very low mark.

I win:you win – This is what you should be aiming for, both parties gaining from the negotiation. The outcome may not necessarily benefit both equitably but there are positive outcomes for each. The great thing about getting to **win:win** is that it preserves the relationship.

You will have no problems negotiating with this person again and that builds a solid foundation to your future working relationship – and this is why you should be aiming for this outcome.

Remember that there must be some 'non-negotiables' as well as some 'concessions' – tease out these to find out where commonalities can be accommodated easily. Also try to ascertain links. For example if there is only a small pot of money and you all want to undertake training programmes, do any of the projects link in any way? Can you share the money by sharing the training? Finally think about creative solutions. What could you get for free? The room? The trainer? Lunch? Can any of it be provided in a different format? Webinars? E-learning? All of these would bring down the cost of the training programme.

Now, let's move onto the final stage of the assessment centre: the interview.

Chapter 6
Assessment
Centre Interview

Generally, you will need to take two interviews in order to gain a place as a crime scene investigator. The first of these interviews will be taken at the assessment centre. It will last for 20 minutes, and will consist of 4 competency-based questions. The second interview will be taken after the assessment centre. This will be a longer interview, and more focused around getting to know you and your motivations for joining the police. In this chapter, we are going to cover both stages of the interview in one go. We'll start off with the competency-based questions, before moving onto questions that you can expect to hear during the second interview.

The Assessment Centre Interview

The assessment centre interview is structured, and will take 20 minutes to complete. The interview panel will consist of two or three people. These can be from either the uniformed side of the service or support staff. You will be asked 4 questions in total. The **first two questions** will be focused on your **values and motivation** for joining the police, and the **last two questions** will focus on your **past experience and ability to demonstrate the core competencies**. These final 2 questions are known as **situational questions**. You will be given a total of 5 minutes to answer each of the 4 questions. The person interviewing you will stop you if you go over the five minutes. As the person interviewing you asks you the question, they will also give you a written copy of the question to refer to. When you consider your responses to the interview questions, you should only choose examples that you feel comfortable discussing with the person interviewing you.

It is important to remember that whilst you will be nervous you should try not to let this get in the way of your success. Treat the interview no differently to this. You ARE capable of becoming a crime scene investigator, and the nerves that you have on the day are only natural, in fact they will help you to perform better if you have prepared sufficiently. The crucial element to your success, as with the rest of the selection process, is your preparation.

The interview board will have a number of set questions to choose from. Whilst these are constantly changing, they will usually form part of the police core competencies. Before attending your interview, ensure that you read, digest and understand the police core competencies. Without these it will be difficult to pass the interview. Even when answering the values and motivations questions, it is important to make sure that you are still using the core competencies.

The person who interviews you will assess your responses against the type of behaviours you need to perform effectively in the role. You must make sure that you are familiar with the competencies and that your answer gives you an opportunity to explain how you have shown this behaviour. As a refresh, the competencies that you will need to be familiar with are:

- Service Delivery;

- Serving the Public;

- Professionalism;

- Working with Others.

While some of these competencies might not be directly relevant to the role of a crime scene investigator, it's important for the police to know that you share their ethos and core beliefs. Since you are still employed by the police in a crime scene investigating capacity, it's fundamental that you can share and demonstrate their values.

You will also be assessed on the quality of your oral communication throughout the interview. Along with all of this, you should **try your best** to show a knowledge and understanding of the crime scene investigator specific core competencies/behavioural requirements. These are:

- Attention to Detail;

- Communication and Teamwork;

- Organisation;

- Composure;

- Analytical Skills;

- Accuracy.

Essentially, you'll need to demonstrate the police core competencies as much as you can throughout the 4 interview questions. In the second interview that you take, the crime scene investigator specific core competencies will be more important.

How to Answer Situational Questions

During the interview, the panel will ask you questions that relate to how you have previously responded or acted in a given situation. This type of question is called a 'situational' type question.

Your response to each situational question must be 'specific' in nature. This means that you must provide an example where you have already been in this type of situation. During your response, you should provide details of how you handled or dealt with the situation, preferably with a successful outcome.

Do not fall into the trap of providing a 'generic' response that details what you 'would do' if the situation arose, unless of course you have not been in this type of situation before. When responding to situational questions try to structure your responses in a logical and concise manner. The way to achieve this is to use the 'STAR' method of interview question response construction.

How to Improve Your Oral Communication

Whilst you will not normally be questioned directly in relation to oral communication during the interview, you will be assessed indirectly.

During the assessment centre competency-based interview, the panel will be looking to see how you communicate and also how you structure your responses to the interview questions.

Consider the following points both during the interview, and whilst responding to the interview questions:

• When you walk into the interview room, stand up straight and introduce yourself. Be polite and courteous at all times and try to come across in a pleasant manner. The panel will be assessing you as soon as you walk through the door so make sure you make a positive first impression.

• Do not sit down in the interview chair until you are invited to do so. This is good manners.

• When you sit down in the interview chair, sit up straight and do not fidget or slouch. It is acceptable to use hand gestures when explaining your responses to the questions but don't overdo it, as they can become a distraction.

• Structure your responses to the questions in a logical manner – this is very important. When responding to an interview question, start at the beginning and work your way through in a concise manner, and at a pace that is easy for the panel to listen to.

• Speak clearly and in a tone that is easy for the panel to hear. Be confident in your responses.

• When talking to the panel use eye contact but be careful not to look at them in an intimidating manner.

• Consider wearing some form of formal outfit to the interview such as a suit. Whilst you will not be assessed on the type of outfit you wear to the interview, it will make you come across in a more professional manner.

Preparing for the Assessment Centre Interview

When preparing for the assessment centre competency-based interview, you should try to formulate responses to questions that surround the assessable core competencies.

The responses that you provide should be specific examples of where you have been in that particular scenario. In your 'welcome pack', which will be sent to you approximately 2 weeks before the date of your assessment centre, you should find examples of the 'core competencies'. For example, one of the sections you will be assessed against could be 'Working with Others'. You may be asked a question where you have to give an example of where you worked effectively as part of a team in order to achieve a difficult task or goal. Try to think of an example where you have had to do this and structure your answer around the core competencies required, e.g. you worked cooperatively with the others, supported the rest of the team members and persuaded them to follow your ideas for completing the task.

On the following page I have provided you with an example of how your response could be structured if you were responding to a question that was based around the core competency of professionalism.

Remember that the following sample question and response is for example purposes only.

SAMPLE INTERVIEW QUESTION BASED AROUND THE CORE COMPETENCY OF PROFESSIONALISM.

Question – Please provide an example of where you have taken responsibility to resolve a problem?

"After reading an appeal in my local paper from a local charity I decided to try to raise money for this worthwhile cause by organising a charity car wash day at the local school during the summer holidays. I decided that the event would take place in a month's time, which would give me enough time to organise such an event. The head teacher at the school agreed to support me during the organisation of the event and provide me with the necessary resources required to make it a success.

I set about organising the event and soon realised that I had made a mistake in trying to arrange everything on my own, so I arranged for two of my work colleagues to assist me.

Once they had agreed to help me I started out by providing them with a brief of what I wanted them to do. I informed them that, in order for the event to be a success, we needed to act with integrity and profession-alism at all times. I then asked one of them to organise the booking of the school and arrange local sponsorship in the form of buckets, sponges and car wash soap to use on the day, so that we did not have to use our own personal money to buy them. I asked the second person to arrange advertising in the local newspaper and radio stations so that we could let the local community know about our charity car wash event, which would in turn hopefully bring in more money on the day for the charity.

Following a successful advertising campaign, I was inundated with calls from local newspapers about our event and it was becoming hard work having to keep talking to them and explaining what the event was all about. But I knew that this information was important if we were to raise our target of £500.

Everything was going well right up to the morning of the event, when I realised we had not got the key to open the school gates. It was the summer holidays so the caretaker was not there to open the gates for us. Not wanting to let everyone down, I jumped in my car and made my way down to the caretaker's house and managed to wake him up and get the key just in time before the car wash event was due to start.

In the end the day was a great success and we all managed to raise £600 for the local charity. Throughout the event I put in lots of extra effort in order to make it a great success. Once the event was over I decided to ask the head teacher for feedback on how he thought I had managed the project. He provided me with some excellent feedback and some good pointers for how I might improve in the future when organising events. I took on-board his feedback in order to improve my skills."

Now that we have taken a look at a sample response, let's explore how the response matched the core competency.

HOW THE RESPONSE MATCHES THE CORE COMPETENCY BEING ASSESSED

In order to demonstrate how effective the above response is, we have broken it down into sections, and provided the core competency area that it matches.

"...I decided to try to raise money for this worthwhile cause by organising a charity car wash day..."

Core competency matched:

• Acts with integrity.

• Uses own initiative.

"Once they had agreed to help me I started out by providing them with a brief of what I wanted them to do. I informed them that, in order for the event to be a success, we needed to act with integrity and professionalism at all times."

Core competency matched:

• Acting with integrity and demonstrating a strong work ethic.

"...which would give me enough time to organise such an event."

Core competency matched:

• Takes ownership.

"I set about organising the event and soon realised that I had made a mistake in trying to arrange everything on my own, so I arranged for 2 of my work colleagues to

assist me."

Core competency matched:

• Takes ownership.

• Uses initiative.

"...arrange local sponsorship in the form of buckets, sponges and car wash soap to use on the day, so that we did not have to use our own personal money to buy them."

Core competency matched:

• Uses initiative.

"Once the event was over I decided to ask the head teacher for feedback on how he thought I had managed the project. He provided me with some excellent feedback and some good pointers for how I might improve in the future when organising events. I took on-board his feedback in order to improve my skills."

Core competency matched:

• Asks for and acts on feedback.

"Following a successful advertising campaign, I was inundated with calls from local newspapers about our event and it was becoming hard work having to keep talking to them and explaining what the event was all about. But I knew that this information was important if we were to raise our target of £500."

Core competency matched:

• Uses initiative.

"Not wanting to let everyone down, I jumped in my car and made my way down to the caretaker's house and managed to wake him up and get the key just in time before the car wash event was due to start."

Core competency matched:

• Uses initiative.

• Takes ownership.

• Showing a strong work ethic.

The explanations above have hopefully highlighted the importance of matching the core competencies that are being assessed.

When you receive your 'Welcome Pack', make sure you read it thoroughly and prepare yourself fully for the interview. Preparation is everything and by reading exactly what is required you will increase your chances of success on the day.

On the following pages, we have provided you with a number of sample assessment centre interview questions that are based around the core competencies. Following each question we have provided you with some useful tips and advice on how you may consider answering the question. For the purposes of this exercise, we have simply provided you with competency based questions. When we show you how to answer the final interview questions, we'll give you some great tips on how to answer motivations and value type questions, and provide you with full sample responses to each and every single question.

SAMPLE COMPETENCY-BASED INTERVIEW QUESTION 1 (WORKING WITH OTHERS)

Please provide an example of where you have worked as part of a team to achieve a difficult task.

Tips for constructing your response:

• Try to think of a situation where you volunteered to work with a team in order to achieve a difficult task. It is better to say that you volunteered as opposed to being asked to get involved by another person.

• Those candidates who can provide an example where they achieved the task despite the constraints of time will generally score better.

• Consider structuring your response in the following manner:

STEP 1 – Explain what the situation was and how you became involved.

STEP 2 – Now explain who else was involved and what the task was.

STEP 3 – Explain why the task was difficult and whether there were any time constraints.

STEP 4 – Explain how it was decided who would carry out what task.

STEP 5 – Now explain what had to be done and how you overcame any obstacles or hurdles.

STEP 6 – Explain what the result/outcome was. Try to make the result positive as a result of your actions.

Now use the template on the following page to construct your own response to this question based on your own experiences and knowledge.

Sample competency-based interview question 1

Please provide an example of where you have worked as part of a team to achieve a difficult task.

Examples of probing questions:

1. Would you have done anything different next time?

2. How did the end result make you feel?

SAMPLE COMPETENCY-BASED INTERVIEW QUESTION 2 (PROFESSIONALISM)

Provide an example of where you have challenged someone's behaviour that was either discriminatory or inappropriate. What did you do and what did you say?

Tips for constructing your response:

• Read carefully the core competency that relates to respect for race and diversity before constructing your response.

• When challenging this type of behaviour, make sure you remain calm at all times and never become aggressive or confrontational.

Consider structuring your response in the following manner:

STEP 1 – Explain what the situation was and how you became involved.

STEP 2 – Now explain who else was involved and why you felt that the behaviour was inappropriate or discriminatory. What was it that was being said or done?

STEP 3 – Now explain what you said or did and why.

STEP 4 – Explain how the other person/people reacted when you challenged the behaviour.

STEP 5 – Now explain what the end result was. Try to make the result positive following your actions.

STEP 6 – Finally explain why you think it was that the people/ person behaved as they did.

Now use the template on the following page to construct your own response to this question based on your own experiences and knowledge.

Sample competency-based interview question 2

Provide an example of where you have challenged someone's behaviour that was either discriminatory or inappropriate. What did you do and what did you say?

Examples of probing questions

1. How did you feel when you were challenging their behaviour?

2. How did the person or people react when you challenged their behaviour?

SAMPLE COMPETENCY-BASED INTERVIEW QUESTION 3 (SERVING THE PUBLIC)

Provide an example of where you have broken down barriers between a group of people.

Tips for constructing your response:

• Read carefully the core competency that relates to serving the public.

• Try to include keywords and phrases from the core competency in your response to this question, such as: "I tried to understand each person's needs and concerns." "I took steps to identify the best way that we could all work together."

"I had their best interests at heart throughout."

"I built confidence in them by talking to them."

Consider structuring your response in the following manner:

STEP 1 – Explain what the situation was and why you needed to break down the barriers.

STEP 2 – Now explain what steps you took in order to achieve the goal.

STEP 3 – Now explain why you took that particular action, and also the thought process behind your actions.

STEP 4 – Explain the barriers or difficulties that you had to overcome in order to achieve the task/objective.

STEP 5 – Now explain what the end result was. Try to

make the result sound positive following your actions.

Now use the template on the following page to construct your own response to this question based on your own experiences and knowledge.

Sample competency-based interview question 3

Provide an example of where you have broken down barriers between a group of people.

Examples of probing questions:

1. What did you learn from this experience and would you do anything differently next time?

2. What did the other people think about what you did? Were they happy with your work?

SAMPLE COMPETENCY-BASED INTERVIEW QUESTION 4 (SERVICE DELIVERY)

Please provide an example of where you have organised a difficult task effectively.

Tips for constructing your response:

• Read carefully the core competency that relates to service delivery.

• Try to include keywords and phrases from the core competency in your response to this question.

• Consider structuring your response in the following manner:

STEP 1 – Explain what the situation was and what it was you needed to organise.

STEP 2 – Now explain why the task was so difficult.

STEP 3 – Now explain what you did and why you did it. Also explain your considerations when organising the task.

STEP 4 – Explain what problems you had and how you overcame them.

STEP 5 – Finally explain what the end result was. Try to provide a positive outcome to the situation.

Now use the template on the following page to construct your own response to this question based on your own experiences and knowledge.

Sample competency-based interview question 4

Please provide an example of where you have organised a difficult task effectively.

Examples of probing questions:

1. What did you learn from this experience and would you do anything differently next time?

2. Why do you think the task was so difficult?

MORE SAMPLE QUESTIONS TO PREPARE FOR BASED ON THE CORE COMPETENCIES

In this short section, we will provide you with a number of sample interview questions to prepare for, in relation to the core competencies.

SERVICE DELIVERY

Q. Give an example of when you have worked towards an organisations objectives or priorities.

Q. Give an example of when you have planned and organised a difficult task.

Q. Give an example of when you have carried out many different tasks at once.

Q. Give me an example of when you have sought advice from others whilst carrying out a difficult work-related task.

SERVING THE PUBLIC

Q. Give an example of when you have provided excellent customer service.

Q. Give me an example of when you have addressed someone else's needs or expectations.

Q. Give me an example of when you have broken down barriers amongst a group of people.

Q. Give an example of when you have worked with another person or group of people to deliver an excellent level of service.

PROFESSIONALISM

Q. Give an example of when you have worked in accordance with an organisation's standards or ethics.

Q. Give an example of when you have taken ownership of a particular problem.

Q. Give an example of when you have acted on your own initiative to resolve an issue or difficult problem.

Q. Give an example of when you have challenged someone's behaviour which was discriminatory of inappropriate.

Q. Give an example of when you have acted on feedback which has been supplied by someone else.

Q. Give me an example of when you have resolved a difficult situation in a calm manner.

Q. Give me an example of when you have defused a potentially hostile situation.

WORKING WITH OTHERS

Q. Give an example of when you have supported other members of a team.

Q. Give an example of when you have worked with other people to achieve a difficult task.

Q. Give an example of when you have briefed a team in relation to a difficult task which had to be achieved.

Q. Give an example of when you have persuaded a group of people to follow your course of action or plan.

Q. Give an example of when you have treated a person or group of people with dignity and respect.

Now, let's move onto the final interview.

Chapter 7
Final Interview

Following the assessment centre, you will face a short wait to find out whether you have been successful. If you are successful, then you will be invited to attend a final interview. This interview will usually be held at the constabulary's headquarters, and will be taken with two or three senior members of the law enforcement team.

If you have reached this point, congratulations. The police are seriously interested in hiring you to become a crime scene investigator. However, this is no time to relax. In order to pass the final interview, you will need to demonstrate to the police that you are enthusiastic, dedicated and hardworking. In this chapter, we'll take you through the final interview, and give you in-depth sample responses for some of the potential questions that you might encounter at this stage.

What's the difference between this interview, and the last interview?

At the assessment centre, you will have faced a rigorously timed and relentlessly structured interview. The final interview is a little bit more relaxed, and perhaps a bit less intimidating. Here, the focus is just as much on getting to know you as a person and a potential employee, as it is on the core competencies. The interview can range from between half an hour to an hour, and will focus on issues such as why you have applied to become a crime scene investigator, why you have applied to that force in particular and what you know about the role. You'll also be asked some more competency-based questions.

Along with this, you can expect the final CSI interview to focus more heavily on the competencies specific to crime scene investigating than the previous. While the assessment centre interview is about establishing that you meet the police core values and expectations, this interview will require you to demonstrate to the interviewer that you have the qualities needed to become a great CSI.

Let's take a refresh on what these qualities are:

- Attention to Detail;

- Communication and Teamwork;

- Organisation;

- Composure;

- Analytical Skills;

- Accuracy.

The better you can demonstrate these qualities, the higher your chances of success will be.

How to Prepare for the Final Interview

If you have made it this far in the selection process, then you have done tremendously well. The Police Service are certainly interested in recruiting you but they want to find out more about you first. There are a number of areas that you will need to prepare for and these are as follows:

1. Interview technique.

2. The reasons why you want to become a crime scene investigator and what you know about the role.

3. What you know about the service you are applying to join.

4. Situational interview questions.

In the previous chapter, we covered how to prepare for situational interview questions in great detail. Now that we know this, let's break down the other areas in detail.

INTERVIEW TECHNIQUE

Many candidates spend little or no time improving or developing their interview technique. It is important that you spend sufficient time on this area, as it will allow your confidence to improve.

The way to improve interview technique is to carry out what we call a mock interview. Mock interviews are where you ask a friend or relative to ask you a number of interview questions under formalised interview conditions. This can be achieved at home across your dining room table or even whilst sat on the chairs in your living room.

During the mock interview you should work on your interview technique. The mock interview will also give you a valuable opportunity to try out your responses to a number of sample interview questions that are contained within this guide. It is important that your mock interviewer provides you with constructive feedback. Do not choose somebody who will tell you that you were great, even when you weren't, as this just defeats the whole purpose of a mock interview.

CARRYING OUT A MOCK INTERVIEW

• Choose a quiet room in the house or at another suitable location.

• Set the room up with a table and two chairs.

• The interviewer then invites you into the room and the interview commences. Don't forget to be polite and courteous to the interviewer and only sit down when invited to do so.

• When the interviewer asks you the questions, respond to them in a logical manner and in a tone of voice that can be easily heard.

• Throughout the mock interview work hard on your technique and style. Sit upright at all times and look at the interviewer using soft eye contact. Do not fidget or slouch in the interview chair.

• Once the interview is over, ask the interviewer for feedback on your performance.

• Repeat the process at least three times until you are comfortable with your technique and style of answering.

<u>The reasons why you want to become a crime scene investigator, and what you know about the role.</u>

During the final interview the panel may ask you questions that relate to why you want to become a crime scene investigator, and in particular what you know about the role.

In the build-up to your interview you need to think

carefully about why you want to become a CSI and what it is exactly that has attracted you to the role. Those candidates who want to become a crime scene investigator so that they can 'see dead bodies' and 'look cool' will score poorly. Only you will know the exact reasons why you want to join the police, but here are some examples of good reasons, and examples of poor reasons.

Good reasons to give:

• To make a difference to your community, and make it a safer place, by helping to solve crime.

• To carry out a job that is worthwhile and one that makes a difference.

• The variety of the job and the different things that you will see on a daily basis.

• The chance to work with a highly professional team that is committed to achieving the values and principles of the service.

• The opportunity to learn new skills.

Poor reasons to give:

• The pay and pension.

• The leave or holiday that you will get.

• Wearing a uniform, which ultimately means you don't

have to pay for your own work clothes.

• Catching criminals and driving a police car.

What do you know about the role?

After studying this guide you will know a considerable amount about the role of a police officer. Before the final interview, you must carry out plenty of research into the role and what the service will expect of you as a serving police officer.

Remember that the role is predominantly based around the core competencies, so be fully familiar with them before you attend the interview. It is also advisable that you study your recruitment literature and also the website of the service you are applying to join.

What do you know about the constabulary that you are applying to join?

During the final interview, there is a strong possibility that you will be asked questions that relate to the service you are applying to join.

The following sample questions are the types that have been asked during final interviews in the past:

Q. What is it that has attracted you to this particular constabulary?

Q. What can you tell me about the structure of this constabulary?

Q. What can you tell me about the geographical area of this Police Service?

Q. Can you tell me how this constabulary is doing in relation to crime reduction?

Q. What crime reduction activities is this constabulary currently involved in?

Q. What are the ambitions of this Police Service?

Q. Who are our partners and stakeholders?

In order to prepare for questions that relate to the service you are applying to join, your first port of call is their website. From here you will be able to find out a considerable amount of information about their structure and activities and their success in driving down crime.

You may also wish to consider contacting your local police station and asking if it is possible to talk to a serving police officer about his or her role and the activities that the service are currently engaged in.

Now, let's move onto looking at some interview questions and answers!

Sample Interview Question 1

Tell us why you want to become a crime scene investigator.

In this question, the interviewer is trying to find out your motivation for becoming a crime scene investigator. It's important for the police to establish that you are applying for the right reasons. Remember that this is an extremely difficult job, where you will be faced with tough scenarios, and therefore they don't want to hire someone who will drop out on the first day. They need someone dedicated and committed, who is prepared to give their all to the position. You should acknowledge the difficulty of the role in your response, but make it clear that you are more than prepared for the challenges you will face, and welcome them. Along with this, you could also tell them about your current role, and why you want to leave. Make sure you are really positive though. Being negative about your current employer will not create a good impression.

Have a go at creating your own response to this question, using the textbox on the next page. Then, compare it to our sample answer.

Your Response

<u>Sample Response</u>

I am extremely enthusiastic about the prospect of becoming a crime scene investigator. Although I have worked in my current role now for a number of years, and have a fantastic employer, I no longer feel challenged by this role. I fully understand that working as a crime scene investigator is a tough and emotional role, but I really believe that I have the qualities to thrive in this position.

Along with working for the police, a hugely respected organisation, I am someone who is extremely analytical, accurate and precise in everything that I do. I studied forensic science at university, and therefore I already have a fantastic depth of CSI knowledge. I feel confident that with minimal training, I can step into any crime scene and perform a great job on behalf of your constabulary.

Finally, it goes without saying that I have a huge interest in crime and law enforcement. I have always been fascinated by the technical details of crime scene investigation work, and I believe this job will really fulfil that natural interest.

I believe that I have the right qualities for this role, and to help your constabulary deliver a fantastic service to the public.

Sample Interview Question 2

Tell us why you want to work for this constabulary in particular, as a crime scene investigator.

In this question, the interviewer is trying to establish what you already know about the constabulary that you are applying for. When we say 'establish what you already know', we mean that you SHOULD know a great deal of information about them. Prior to the interview, you should have conducted as much research as you can about the constabulary. This includes information such as what problems the force are currently dealing with, the way in which they police your local area and anything else you can find out. The more info you can give, the better. This tells the interview two things. Firstly, it shows that you have a genuine interest in the role. If you have not researched prior, and can't give a good response to this, then you will come across as uninterested and unenthusiastic. Secondly, it shows that you are someone who is organised and prepared. By conducting prior research, you have already demonstrated one of the crime scene investigator core competencies – organisation. Thus, the interviewer will get a great impression of you.

Have a go at creating your own response to this question, using the textbox on the next page. Then, compare it to our sample answer.

Your Response

Sample Response

Prior to applying for this job, I conducted a great deal of research into this constabulary, and I was really impressed with what I found. Having grown up in the same town, I am already aware of the fantastic work that your constabulary performs on a daily basis, but my research showed me just how impressive this work is. For example, I was not aware that in the last 2 years alone, the work performed by your officers has resulted in a local crime rate reduction of over 30%. This is an enormous figure, and I would be honoured to work for an organisation who can boast such stats.

Along with this, I also spoke to serving members of your constabulary, to enquire as to what it is like working for you. I received extremely positive feedback from everyone that I spoke to. Every single person told me that working for Ficshire Police provides them with a challenging and highly professional environment to work in, and that the constabulary is highly committed to working together as a team. This is inspiring to me, and really motivated me to apply. I would love to work in a team as respectable as yours, and I hope you'll consider me for this position.

Sample Interview Question 3

What are your biggest strengths?

This is a very common interview question, and therefore is one that you should prepare for. Be careful when answering this question, as you don't want to come across in the wrong way. The best answer to this question will be a reserved response, which does not fall short on informing the interviewer of your qualities. Ideally, pick two qualities (which match the core competencies) and then elaborate on them. Try not to go too overboard, but at the same time, make sure you show the interviewer how capable you are. Don't forget to back your strengths up with examples too, giving the interviewer a description of a time when you have used these skills.

Have a go at creating your own response to this question, using the textbox on the next page. Then, compare it to our sample answer.

Your Response

Sample Response

I would say that my biggest strengths are my attention to detail and my composure when under pressure.

In regards to attention to detail, this is a skill that I have used and honed throughout my career, and has aided me greatly in a professional capacity. As a forensic science student, my attention to detail was key to helping me pass my course at university, and I worked fastidiously to ensure that this was always on point. As a result, I completed my degree with first class honours, which I believe was a testament to my attention to detail. Following this, I used my attention to detail in a role as a financial advisor, for a hugely respectable company. I produced fantastic results for this company, and frequently produced monthly high records in customer satisfaction. I understand that attention to detail is really essential for crime scene investigators, who need to be able to spot minor details, which could prove essential to the case.

Along with this, I take great pride in my ability to remain calm under pressure. I feel that this was particularly evident during my last role, where I was working in a busy restaurant. As shift leader, I was required to manage and organise other staff members under often difficult conditions. Working in a restaurant, particularly as a shift leader, is extremely demanding. You need to be organised, calm and efficient, and I am pleased to say that I fully demonstrated my prowess in all of these areas. I understand that composure is vital for crime scene investigators, who are often faced with difficult scenarios. I am more than ready to deal with this, and I know that I can maintain my composure, regardless of what comes my way.

Sample Interview Question 4

What do you understand the term 'integrity' to mean?

This is a question which challenges you directly on one of the police core values – integrity. If you find this unusual, then you need to take a look over the competencies. Integrity means treating every single person that you meet with respect and fairness, and taking a professional approach at all times. You must be honest and responsible too. It's imperative that every single employee of the police acts with the utmost integrity at all times. Regardless of whether you are an officer or a crime scene investigator, you are still a member of law enforcement and therefore you have a job to set an example for the public.

With all of this in mind, it should be fairly simple to answer this question. You need to show the interviewer that you fully believe in integrity, and that you have a good understanding of the qualities that are linked with it – such as professionalism.

Have a go at creating your own response to this question, using the textbox on the next page. Then, compare it to our sample answer.

Your Response

Sample Response

I consider myself to be someone who acts with integrity at all times, and I believe this is a fundamental quality for a person to have. For me, integrity refers to the core concepts of honesty, professionalism and fairness. This is especially important for members of the police force. Regardless of the capacity in which they are working, it's imperative that police employees can set a great example to the public. The best way to do this, is through acting with integrity at all times. These are qualities that every single member of law enforcement should seek to exude.

I believe that I am someone who strongly reflects the values of the police. I treat every single person that I meet with respect and fairness, and I believe strongly in the idea that you should treat others in the same way that you yourself would like to be treated. Crime scene investigators should behave to the exact same standards as any other police employee, regardless of how often they will be dealing with the public, and therefore integrity is an essential quality to have.

Sample Interview Question 5

Can you give me an example of a time when you have demonstrated your attention to detail?

This is a situational question, and requires you to recount a previous example of when you have demonstrated a certain behaviour, just as you did in the competency based interview. When answering this, remember to take a really structured approach. Using the STAR method, clearly list the situation, task, action and end result of the scenario; making sure that the end result is as positive as possible due to the actions that you took. Don't be surprised if the interviewers question you from time to time throughout this question, to clarify things. This isn't like the structured interview, and the format is more relaxed, so you'll be free to take a more conversational approach to this question.

Have a go at creating your own response to this question, using the textbox on the next page. Then, compare it to our sample answer.

<u>Your Response</u>

Sample Response

When I was working as a financial advisor at my previous company, I was required to use my attention to detail on a daily basis.

One such occasion that I can remember, was when I was confronted with a very difficult customer. The man in question was extremely unhappy with the service that another advisor had provided him, and claimed that he had been direct-debited for far more than he had originally agreed.

When the man arrived to see me, he was extremely angry. I calmly asked him to take a seat, and then brought him a cup of tea. This seemed to relax him a little, and he eventually explained to me what the problem was. After clarifying the issue, I left the man for a brief period of time, whilst I went to consult with the colleague whom had charged him in the first place. This colleague was adamant that she had not made any mistakes, and told me that she would email me a spreadsheet to confirm this.

When I arrived back at my desk, I opened the spreadsheet to have a look at the charges that had been issued against the man's card. Nothing appeared to be out of the ordinary, and it seemed as if the right payment had been taken. However, upon closer inspection, I noticed that one of the excel formulas was incorrect. This was only a minute detail, but it made a huge difference to the amount of money being taken. It became apparent to me that there had been a mistake.

I immediately turned to the man and apologised to him, citing the error on our part. I offered him a full refund and a free consultation, courtesy of the company. The man was very pleased with this resolution, and left happy.

I believe that in this case, my attention to detail resolved a difficult issue. Had I not spotted this, and continued to insist that the correct charges had been made, the man would have been even more distressed and upset; and this would have reflected badly on the company.

Sample Interview Question 6

Flexibility is really important for crime scene investigators. Would you say you are a flexible person? If so, how do you think it will help you in this role?

This question has two answers. Firstly, yes, you are a flexible person! Secondly, you need to tell them why flexibility is important for a CSI. This is the interviewer testing your knowledge of the role, so show them how much you have learned. As you know, crime scene investigators are required to work shifts, and often work unsociable hours – including weekends. Once a crime has been discovered, it's imperative that investigators are on the scene as soon as possible, in order to recover essential evidence – before it gets contaminated by the environment. Along with this, crime scene investigators also need to be flexible in regards to the type of scenarios they will encounter. It's difficult to prepare yourself for a day's work, as there are so many different scenarios that you might encounter. One day you might be investigating a homicide, the next you might be investigating a burglary or arson. As long as you are prepared to deal with all different types of crime, you are sure to make a great investigator.

Have a go at creating your own response to this question, using the textbox on the next page. Then, compare it to our sample answer.

Your Response

Sample Response

I'm a highly flexible person, and I'm totally prepared to make sacrifices for this job if necessary. I know from my research that crime scene investigators are required to work shift patterns, which may sometimes be at unsociable hours. This is not a problem for me. I'm very familiar with working shifts, from previous positions, and I have often worked night shifts in the past. This means that I'm up for anything, and the idea of being on call whenever the police need me is actually fairly exciting to me. I'm someone who will put my all into this position, and that means giving this job absolute maximum commitment.

Furthermore, I also understand that CSIs are required to take a flexible approach to the actual work that they do too. I know that CSIs are required to work on many different types of cases, ranging from burglary to homicide, but the idea of working in such a changeable environment does not phase me. If anything, I believe this will be a great source of motivation for me, and I'm looking forward to tackling new challenges as and when they arise.

Sample Interview Question 7

Based on what you know about the role, do you think there are any requirements to this role that you might struggle with? If so, which?

This is a very similar question to something which you may have heard in previous interviews – 'what is your biggest weakness?' Just as you would when answering that particular question, you will need to be very careful when responding to this. The difference, of course, is that this is a crime scene investigator specific question – so you need to demonstrate your knowledge of the role too. There is nothing wrong with giving a response along the lines of, 'I have researched the role in-depth and I am very confident in my ability to succeed in all areas,' but at the same time, there is a risk that this could come across as brash or arrogant. Crime scene investigation is extremely difficult. Even the best new recruits will have problems with some areas of the job, it's certainly not a walk in the park, so be as honest as you can be without making yourself sound like a weak candidate. The best way to answer this question is to take a minor weakness, and then elaborate on how you are working to improve it.

Have a go at creating your own response to this question, using the textbox on the next page. Then, compare it to our sample answer.

Your Response

Sample Response

While I am fairly confident in my ability to excel in this role, I do acknowledge that this will be a difficult job to get to grips with. In particular, I believe that it will initially be tough for me to interact with and investigate homicide cases.

That being said, I don't believe that I am abnormally sensitive to such things, and I fully believe that with some training and experience, I'll be ready to take on these cases in no time at all.

I'm fully prepared to put myself out of my comfort zone to succeed in this job, and dealing with uncomfortable scenarios is no exception.

Chapter 8
A Day in The Life
of a CSI

Now that we've covered the main application steps, let's get into some serious detail about the day-to-day activities of a crime scene investigator. In this chapter, we've teamed up with a real life crime scene investigator, to run through a typical working day in his life. For the purposes of this exercise, we'll refer to our CSI as Neil.

DID YOU KNOW?

Scientific ear investigation goes back hundreds of years. Alphonse Bertillon is one of the best-known pioneers in this field.

Neil has been working as a CSI for around 14 years now. He works in a major city, and therefore has experience of dealing with every kind of crime that you could imagine. From homicide to arson, drug dealing to burglary, Neil has been there and investigated it all. Now, he's going to show you what it's really like to work as a CSI. Let's get started!

Neil's Day

6am

Neil gets out of bed at 6am, makes himself some breakfast, goes for a run and then has a shower. Although he is not expected to arrive at the office until 9am (when his first shift starts), he claims it's always important to be up early when working as a CSI.

'Obviously, you need your sleep, but I find that being up early and awake at least a few hours before I'm due to start, helps me concentrate. Likewise, it's important to

stay physically fit. Physical fitness helps to keep your mind sharp, and that is extremely valuable in this job.

It's no good just rolling out of bed and heading straight to the office either. By the time you arrive at your first crime scene, you'll be too tired and make mistakes. The more awake you are, the better.'

8:30am

Neil leaves the house at 8:30am, and arrives at the office at about 8:45. Although he is not expected to be in till 9, it's good to be organised.

'I never turn up for work 'on time'. I'm always early, every single day. You can't just turn up and then roll off to a crime scene, you need to get your things together, get organised, get prepared, mentally psych yourself up if necessary. These things take time… for me at least 15 minutes.'

At 9am, Neil's colleague is waiting for him outside. They are going straight to a crime scene, in his colleague's van. Neil quickly puts together a flask of water and some food for the pair. As he explains, food and drink is often overlooked, especially when dealing with high profile jobs.

'When you are working a major job, it's fairly common to spend up to 8 hours with just a chocolate bar and a small bottle of water for refreshment. These types of cases don't really give the time for stuff like that, as you have to be collecting evidence and working constantly. This is a struggle for new recruits to deal with, but you

soon get used to it.'

9:30am

Neil and his colleague arrive at the scene, and quickly jump into a police van parked outside the house in question, to change into their overalls. Although Neil is just starting his shift at this location, the police have already been here, and escorted away a murder victim.

Neil enters the house via the backdoor. As he explains, it's important for CSIs to pick their entry routes carefully:

'In this case, we had established (given the evidence) that the front door was the likeliest point of access and then exit for the offender. For this reason, it was better to make sure we didn't disturb any evidence that had been left there, and use another route into the house.'

As Neil enters the house, he lays down stepping plates. Stepping plates are used by CSIs to ensure that the floor doesn't get contaminated by external footprints. Although the investigation is not yet at this stage, and Neil is wearing footwear protectors, it will certainly reach that point in the future. The other thing that Neil notices when he steps in the house, is the smell:

'You get used to it, but the smell of death is always repugnant, even for someone who has been working for as long as me. I know it the second I smell it now, it's unmistakable.'

<u>10am</u>

Neil's initial task is to collect items of interest from the murder room. The murder took place on the 2nd floor of the house, in a bedroom. As Neil takes each step, he lays a plate down. Luckily, the carpet leading up the room has been checked for footprints already, and cleared. As Neil makes his way to the bedroom, he starts to sweat. It's extremely hot in the house, but there's nothing he can do, as he can't take off his uniform. As Neil explains, this is just something that you have to deal with:

'Working as a crime scene investigator is not a job that you do for the comfort. You aren't sat in a nice warm chair, staring at a computer screen. A particularly warm house is the least of your concerns. You'll need to brave the elements, dealing with harsh weather…along with being faced with dead bodies, blood, guts and gore. You just learn to put up with it.'

<u>10:30am</u>

Neil arrives in the bedroom. There is no body, as the victim has been taken away the night before, but there is plenty of evidence that has been left behind. Neil quickly gets down to work. There is blood covering the wall beside the bedside table, and fragments of bone and hair on the mattress, as well as on the floor. To one side of the bed is a large piece of metal, also covered in (now slightly dried) blood. The item is a crowbar. It's the murder weapon.

Neil quickly establishes that the blood patterns on the wall are a result of 'cast off'. This is where blood has transferred from the weapon to a surface (such as wall) whilst it is being moved – in this instance, to hit the victim. In order to analyse the blood patterns properly, the team will call in an expert who specialises in blood spatter analysis.

Along with collecting other evidence, it is Neil's job to collect the murder weapon for analysis. Of course, he can't just pick it up. This would lead to contamination, and hinder the investigation. Neil gets this job out of the way first:

'On this job, my main task was to collect the murder weapon. Although it's also imperative to collect other evidence too, it goes without saying that this is mentally draining work; and you certainly don't want to make mistakes when dealing with the murder weapon, as a result of being tired. Of course, there won't be any mistakes, because I'm trained mentally and physically to handle this. However, we are taught to deal with the number 1 priority first of all, so this is what I did.'

<u>11am</u>

The first thing that Neil does, just before collecting the weapon, is to photograph the weapon in relation to the room. This ensures that even once they have the weapon in their possession, they'll be able to look at the photographs and the position that the weapon was found in, to establish key facts about the case. Neil also takes close up pictures of the weapon itself. When doing this, he uses a special lens:

'When taking close up pictures, we use what is called

a macro lens. This allows us to see details that can't otherwise be spotted by the eyes.'

Neil carefully turns the weapon over, taking off his gloves each time. It's important to ensure that no traces from the weapon end up on the camera itself. Once Neil has photographed the weapon in its entirety, he begins the task of boxing it.

<u>11:30am</u>

In order to seal the weapon, Neil uses a window box. This is a container which has folded side flaps, with tabs, to ensure that the weapon is secured. On the top of the container is a plastic window, which allows for viewing of the weapon, without needing to open the box and expose it:

'You'll find that crime scene investigation is full of these little tricks and shortcuts. Well…not shortcuts, but it might surprise people to learn that there is a certain way we have to do things. This is to avoid contamination. We have to be very particular.'

Now that Neil has the weapon inside the box, he needs to actually secure it. The reason for this is that if the weapon is shifting around whilst travelling, it could become contaminated in some way. In order to do this, Neil places two cable ties (sterilised beforehand) to secure it. He has to be very careful about where he places these ties, as he doesn't want them to disrupt the evidence. Following this, he tapes up the edges of the box, to prevent anything from escaping or getting into the box.

12pm

Now that Neil has finished preserving the weapon, and photographing the weapon in relation to the rest of the room, it's time to start dealing with the rest of the scene. As Neil explains, this is the nasty bit of the job:

'I'm literally on my knees, collecting bits of bone and flesh, and hair, from a stranger's floor. It doesn't get much more gruesome. Every piece of evidence needs to be collected carefully and methodically. In this instance, the victim's face had truly been smashed to pieces. In fact, there was probably more of it on the floor than had left the room in the body bag.'

As Neil collects the evidence, with the assistance of a colleague, they need to take constant trips back and forth out to the van. Each time they do this, they change their white suits. This ensures that they are wearing fresh overalls for every new piece of evidence, and reduces the risk of contamination. Along with this, they also get through an enormous amount of gloves. Given that these are the item most exposed to the evidence, it's imperative that they are changed as much as possible:

'On a scene like this one, I'll probably get through at least 90 pairs of gloves. It's also really tiring going back and forth between the van and the house. This is one of the reasons for why Crime Scene Investigators need to stay physically fit.'

3pm

At 3pm, Neil is assigned to go back to the station. Another CSI will be taking over on his behalf, to help his colleague finish.

Once he arrives back at the station, he only has 2 hours left on his shift. His first task is to file a report on what he's seen during the day. This needs to be extremely detailed, and lay out the fundamentals of the evidence collection, the positioning of evidence etc. Neil is also required to respond to a number of emails. As he explains, CSI work isn't just about being at crime scenes.

'CSIs sometimes have to attend court. That means you'll be provided with the details beforehand, and expected to confirm that you can attend, along with clarifying any evidence you need to recap on with your manager before the date.'

5pm

Finally, at 5pm. Neil finishes his shift. Tomorrow, he'll be back at the crime scene. As he points out though, CSI work does not involve working normal shift patterns:

'On this day, I worked 9-5, but that's an odd occurrence. Since CSI work is shift based, I'll sometimes be working extremely unsociable hours, and sometimes it's much longer than 8 hours per shift. New recruits need to be prepared for this.'

DID YOU KNOW?

The Forensic Science Service codes a product called 'Smartwater'. This is a system which sprays intruders with a unique marking, making them easily identifiable later on.

Chapter 9
Helpful
Organisations

In this section, we'll provide you with some information on useful organisations. CSI workers could end up liaising with many of these organisations whilst working for the police, so it's useful to be aware of who they are.

Association of Chief Police Officers (ACPO)

The ACPO are based in Scotland. They are responsible for formulating policies which have a significant impact on policing all across the UK. They provide important manuals, such as the *ACPO Murder Manual*, which gives instructions on how a murder investigation should be carried out.

Crown Prosecution Service (CPS)

The Crown Prosecution Service works in partnership with the police and government, to ensure that the charging and prosecution of criminals is conducted in a smooth manner. They provide the prosecution in magistrates' courts. The CPS acts in the interests of the public.

The European Police Organisation (Europol)

The European Police Organisation consists of members states from the European Union. It allows members of the Union to share vital intelligence and information, which will lead to criminals who may or may not have escaped abroad being detained.

The Forensic Science Service (FSS)

The Forensic Science Service is used by a great number of constabularies, to analyse evidence and assist with investigations. They employ 2500 staff, based in laboratories around the country, and provide an enormous range of services – such as firearm comparisons and fire debris analysis. They are one of the most popular suppliers for police in England and Wales.

LGC Forensics

LGC Forensics are an alternative provider to the FSS, and operate across the UK. Along with offering forensic services, they also provide advice and guidance for courts and legal professionals, on related matters.

Along with the above two, and a range of other providers, the Scottish Police Laboratories and the Forensic Science Service of Northern Ireland provide specialist services in their respective countries.

Home Office Scientific Development Branch (HOSDB)

The HOSDB consists of a number of scientists, engineers and other police employees, who are responsible for developing technologies that can be used to assist the UK police service. They are an extremely innovative organisation, and are responsible for much of the crime solving technology that UK law enforcement uses today.

National Police Improvement Agency (NPIA)

The NPIA consists of a range of specialist departments, which provide knowledge, skills and training to police officers. They are responsible for the regular re-examination of currently serving officers and employees of the police (including CSIs) and conduct their training and examination at various sites across the country. The NPIA is an essential means for the police to ensure that their staff are efficient and up-to-date with all of the latest requirements.

WHY NOT TAKE A LOOK AT OUR OTHER POLICE GUIDES!

FOR MORE INFORMATION ON OUR POLICE GUIDES, PLEASE CHECK OUT THE FOLLOWING:

WWW.HOW2BECOME.COM

Get Access To

FREE

Psychometric Tests

www.PsychometricTestsOnline.co.uk

Made in the USA
Las Vegas, NV
28 January 2021